W9-BJV-405

"'Great ideas often enter reality in strange guises and with disgusting alliances.' This phrase, from Whitehead's *Adventures of Ideas,* raises intriguing questions about the college youth movement. Should its claim to transform our moral sensibilities and national life styles be taken seriously? Are we witnessing the growth of an authentic and, in the European sense of the word, *serious* movement in American history, or merely a nervous spasm elicited in response to the nervous-making events of our time?"

—Daniel Yankelovich

The survey reported in this book provides interesting background details which should be examined thoughtfully before any evaluation is made of the worth of the ideas being pressed upon our consciousness by student advocates.

This title is available in quantity lots at special discount prices for public service and corporate use. For details, write our Special Projects Agency: The Benjamin Company, 485 Madison Avenue, New York, N. Y. 10022.

THE CHANGING VALUES ON CAMPUS

Political and Personal Attitudes of Today's College Students

A Survey for The JDR 3rd Fund by Daniel Yankelovich, Inc.

Introduction by John D. Rockefeller 3rd

WASHINGTON SQUARE PRESS
POCKET BOOKS · NEW YORK

THE CHANGING VALUES ON CAMPUS

WASHINGTON SQUARE PRESS edition published March, 1972

The 1968 data used in this book are from a survey for *Fortune* in the magazine's issue of January 1969 under the title "A Special Kind of Rebellion," copyright, ©, 1969, by Time, Inc.

The 1969 data are from a CBS News background study for the television program called "Generations Apart," copyright, ©, 1969, by Columbia Broadcasting System, Inc.

The 1970 data are from a report published in February 1971 by the JDR 3rd Fund under the title "Youth and the Establishment."

The charts accompanying the tables in this book were supplied by the Western Electric Company.

Published by
POCKET BOOKS, a division of Simon & Schuster, Inc.,
630 Fifth Avenue, New York, N.Y.

WASHINGTON SQUARE PRESS editions are distributed in the U.S. by Simon & Schuster, Inc., 630 Fifth Avenue, New York, N.Y. 10020 and in Canada by Simon & Schuster of Canada, Ltd., Richmond Hill, Ontario, Canada.

Standard Book Number: 671–48751–5.
Copyright, ©, 1972, by the JDR 3rd Fund, Inc. All rights reserved.
Published on the same day in Canada by Simon & Schuster of Canada, Ltd.,
Richmond Hill, Ontario.
Printed in the U.S.A.

Contents

CONTENTS

CONTENTS

PART II PROFILES

CONTENTS

Introduction

THIS BOOK is offered as a contribution to public understanding of the opinions, attitudes, and general mood of American college youth. It tells much about what young people think of the society they live in. It is especially valuable because the testimony comes from college youth itself. One might say that the real authors of this book are the 1,244 students who gave the answers recorded here.

The JDR 3rd Fund believes that genuine communication between young people and the Establishment is essential for our society. We have felt that communication would be aided by a dispassionate presentation of the actual opinions of college students about some of the key issues of our time. We recognize, of course, that dialogue is not an end in itself, but it may be a means by which effective cooperation can come to pass. An understanding of what youth thinks about the questions of morals, politics, and values dealt with in this survey can be an important step toward meaningful dialogue. That, in turn, *can* lead to effective cooperative action, with important benefits for the participants as well as for society in general.

The Fund was fortunate in being able to engage the services of Daniel Yankelovich, Inc., to carry out this project in the late spring of 1971, and in having Mr. Yankelovich prepare the analysis of the data, as he did in the case of the previous survey, published by the JDR 3rd Fund under the title *Youth and the Establishment*.

In that earlier publication, as in this one, it was possible to combine the new results with data from 1968 and 1969 Yankelovich surveys carried out for *Fortune* and CBS News. We are grateful to both organizations for permitting use of their studies. The present book, as a result, gives us a four-year sweep of information instead of being limited to one year.

After presentation of the survey results in Parts I and II of the book, Mr. Yankelovich contributes, in Part III, the essay "The New Naturalism" with his interpretation of the long-term as well as immediate significance of the results.

Acknowledgments are due to the Task Force on Youth which formulated the basic ideas and specific plans for both the present study and its predecessor. The original Task Force included Richard W. Barrett, John E. Harr, David K. Lelewer, Daniel Yankelovich, and Paul Ylvisaker. In the fall of 1970 the Trustees of the JDR 3rd Fund authorized exploration of the youth field and assumed sponsorship of the Task Force. Besides the original Task Force members and Jerry J. Swift, who now directs the project, others who have worked on it over the longest period have included Steven Haft, Robert McG. Lilley, William Ruder, Datus C. Smith, Jr., and Paul Swift. The JDR 3rd Fund wishes to express its appreciation to Mrs. Ruth Clark, vice president of Daniel Yankelovich, Inc., for her participation in direction of the surveys and analysis of the results.

We on the Task Force on Youth owe our greatest debt to the many people we have come to know in our efforts at stimulating Youth-Establishment dialogue and cooperation. These people—young and old, longhairs and corporate executives—embody and typify the cross-generation and cross-culture collaboration necessary to the well-being of our society.

—JOHN D. ROCKEFELLER 3RD

PART I

The College Scene
1968-1971

CHAPTER 1

Background and Highlights

IN THE MID-1960's observers of the college scene were beginning to sense that something important was happening on American college campuses. By the late 1960's, when campus unrest had moved toward its climax of strikes and confrontations, a flood of books, articles, TV shows, and films appeared interpreting to the public why the most privileged young people in America were so radical, discontented, and alienated.

Few observers remained neutral. Campus events touched too many nerves and aroused too much anxiety (or exhilaration) to permit dispassionate observation. And so, it was scarcely noticed how rare hard facts were in all the lengthy interpretations, denunciations, panegyrics, and diagnoses. Here and there an occasional survey measured attitudes toward Vietnam or counted the radicals, reassuring the country that the mass of students were "just like us." But events moved so quickly that there was hardly time to take sound measure of what was really happening to the beliefs and values of college students. By the standards of European and South American universities, American college campuses had in the past seemed rustically apolitical and sedate. Had these same staid institutions now suddenly become transformed into incubators of political revolution and harbingers of radical social change?

The Daniel Yankelovich organization began to carry out studies on the college student movement as early as 1965. In the first study at that time[1] they were struck by the influence of what might be called the "psychology of affluence." Relationships to affluence divided college students sharply into two camps. In one camp were the Career-Minded students who did not at all take affluence for granted and whose main motive in going to college was to gain its practical bene-

---

[1] *Young Adults: The Threshold Years.* Institute of Life Insurance, 1965.

fits: more earning power, better career opportunities, and a crack at a higher status position in the society. In the other camp were the students who did take affluence for granted and who reached out toward more intangible values, downgrading the traditional emphasis on economic well-being, career, and social position.

In a nationwide survey of college students conducted by Daniel Yankelovich, Inc., for *Fortune* in the fall of 1967, it was learned that a majority of all students throughout the country (56%) fell into the traditional Career-Minded category, while the other 44 per cent belonged in the newer Take-Affluence-for-Granted group. The *Fortune* study, which was published in January 1968 in a special issue of the magazine on youth, explored a broad range of student values on love, marriage, religion, work, savings, success, drugs, technology, authority, and career choice. The most striking finding it revealed was that the wide departure from traditional values seen on campuses was largely confined to the Take-Affluence-for-Granted minority. The "New Values," the research suggested, reflected the well-known psychological principle of a hierarchy of human needs. According to this principle, the hungry man has food, not sex, on his mind; the sex-starved person finds it hard to focus on chitchat with a sexually appealing companion; and the person who enjoys economic security sets a different value on money from that of someone who may be loaded with responsibilities but lacks income. Student emphasis on self-expression, creativity, and freedom from constraints was accompanied by a de-emphasis on money, success, and traditional morality; and both were strongly related to whether or not the student felt he could take the bread-and-butter benefits of college for granted.

In early 1969, CBS News commissioned the Yankelovich organization to design and carry out a study updating the earlier *Fortune* research but also extending the scope of the research to include more information on political values. The CBS News study was used as material for three hour-long documentaries CBS presented to the public in the late spring of 1969. Inevitably, only a tiny fraction of the research found its way into the documentaries, the nature of television not lending itself to the full-scale presentation of research findings.[2]

---

[2] CBS has made portions of the material available in pamphlet form, *Generations Apart*, CBS News, 1969.

Perhaps the main interest of the CBS News study was the light it shed on the so-called generation gap. Contrasting the values of parents and their college age children, the study showed quite convincingly that the generation gap was a half-truth—and a misleading one at that. While many college students held views at odds with those of their parents, their values conflicted even more sharply with the values of other young people in their own generation who were *not* attending college. In other words, the gap within the generation was greater than that between generations. Indeed, the 1969 study showed a strong bond of shared core values between parents and their college age children. Differences were largely confined to the best strategies for achieving shared basic life values.

The 1969 study also showed that the campus had become intensely politicized, many students holding a radical critique of American society and its failings. Although the proportion of out-and-out revolutionaries proved to be small (3%), the number of students who shared some of the revolutionaries' scathing criticisms of our institutions proved to be quite large (approximately 40%, or more than 3 million college students).

Significantly, the 1969 study revealed that while the psychology of affluence has little to do with whether or not a student is a hard-core revolutionary, the main source of sympathy and support for the revolutionary's objectives (if not his methods) come from the large number of students in the Take-Affluence-for-Granted camp. Here it is worth noting that the *psychology* of affluence is independent of affluence itself. That is, students who take affluence for granted do not come from families who are that much richer or better educated or of higher social status than the more career-minded students.

In the following year, 1970, the Yankelovich organization was commissioned by John D. Rockefeller 3rd to conduct a new study of college youth and to compare student values and perspectives with the views of America's business leadership—the chief executive officers of the *Fortune* 500 leading industrial corporations. The central purpose of this study was to ascertain whether, despite the increasingly sharp conflict between college youth and the so-called Establishment, any solid ground existed for collaboration between the two groups in tackling the kinds of problems that students felt most urgently needed attention.

5

The findings of the 1970 study were published in pamphlet form in the fall of that year.[3] The study showed a surprisingly large core of common concerns shared by the business executives and college students. At the same time, the research documented an awesome collection of obstacles, both practical and psychological, that stood in the way of productive Youth/Establishment collaboration. Balancing out the forces working both for and against cooperative effort, the report concluded that despite the formidable character of the obstacles, fruitful cooperation was possible. Following publication of the study, the JDR 3rd Fund supported several experimental projects to put this proposition to a practical test.

The 1970 research findings had shown a sharp increase in college student mistrust, alienation, and despair above the 1968–1969 levels. Yet, as 1971 began, journalists and other observers sensed that an abrupt change of mood had taken hold on campus. *Time* wrote a lead story on the "Cooling of America," and journalistic reports began to abound describing what appeared to be an unexpected return to normalcy.

In recognition of the significance of what was happening and in the interest of capturing a factual record of the unfolding character of the college student movement, the JDR 3rd Fund commissioned the Yankelovich organization to design and carry out a new 1971 study among a comparable national cross-section of college students. In the new study, fielded in March, April, and May 1971, hour-long personal interviews were conducted with more than 1,200 college students, undergraduate and graduate, in 53 colleges and universities throughout the country. The 1971 study included many questions asked in previous studies so that trends could be measured on student life-style values, political values, and values relating to how best to effect desirable social changes. In addition to these comparison questions, the 1971 study added a host of new questions to assess the mood change reported by the mass media and to round out our picture of current student values. A fundamental change had taken place

[3] *Youth and the Establishment,* a report on research for John D. Rockefeller 3rd and The Task Force on Youth by Daniel Yankelovich, Inc. Published by the JDR 3rd Fund, Inc., 1971.

on campus, differing in major respects from the picture presented by the mass media. Given the importance of the change, a preliminary review of the new findings convinced all participants that the research should be made available to the general public in book form. The 1971 study reveals many surprising, even startling, findings; and it documents other points which, while not as surprising, are far-reaching in their significance.

Here is a sampling of some of the significant findings:

1. The Unlinking of Cultural and Political Values

Radical political values and life-style values which traveled together since the mid-1960's had, in 1971, begun to go their separate ways. Changing cultural values—relationships to marriage, authority, religion, work, money, career, sexual morality, and other aspects of the Puritan Ethic—have become more marked and dramatic each year since these measurements began, including 1971, while political beliefs have moved in the opposite direction, away from their 1970 peaks. For example, students in 1971 were less critical of our major institutions—the two-party system, business, the universities, the unions, the Supreme Court, etc.—than they were in the previous year. Nine out of ten students expect to register and to vote in the 1972 Presidential elections. Three out of four believe that desirable social change can best be effected by working within the system. In 1970, two-thirds of the student body thought that student radicalism would continue to grow. A year later a majority believed it is leveling off or declining.

The separation of cultural values from political values has not taken place among students who identify themselves with the New Left (11% in 1971). For these students, the life styles of the counterculture and radical politics go together. But the vast majority of students—the 89 per cent who do not identify with the New Left—have pressed forward in their search for a cultural revolution while taking a step backwards from political revolution.

7

2. A Change of Mood

The mood of personal despair and depression felt by so many students in 1970 was largely dissipated. Perhaps the best single phrase describing the current student mood is, *confused but not despairing.* The shift in mood away from despair and depression does not, however, mean that students feel better about the state of our society; on the contrary, they are more uneasy and worried than a year earlier. More of them think that we have a sick society on our hands than in previous years. Only a handful believe our national policies will lead to peace or economic well-being. And a whopping 30 per cent of all students say they would rather live in some other country than the United States— Australia, Canada or Western Europe being the preferred choices.

Why, then, so abrupt a shift of mood? It would appear that students have sharply divorced their worries about the state of the nation from their own personal fate. Withdrawing emotional involvement from social and political matters, they have channeled their feelings into their own private lives where they experience more control, less frustration . . . and greater contentment.

We can see here the workings of a familiar and powerful mechanism that often shows itself among older groups in the population. People have a limited tolerance for frustration. Why, as the saying goes, continue to knock your head against a stone wall? When the feeling of futility is prolonged and when people can manage to avoid the anxiety it causes, they turn to less frustrating outlets. And when one is young, intelligent, unburdened with responsibilities and surrounded by like-minded friends and lovers, it is not surprising to find a shift away from despair to more satisfying experiences. What is more surprising is the abruptness of the shift.

3. Marxian Spectacles, Capitalist Values

Students today view the society and its workings through Marxian spectacles, but their underlying values are largely those

8

of the traditional free-enterprise system. A majority of students (58%) believe that the real power in the country is vested in big business and the giant financial institutions rather than in the Congress (31%), Presidency (23%), special-interest groups other than business (15%) or public opinion (10%). Furthermore, in true Marxian fashion, the majority (58%) accept the view that our system of government is democratic in name only and that the mass of people are propagandized into believing that what the public thinks really counts.

Coexisting side by side with these classic Marxian precepts, however, is the belief expressed by no fewer than 85 per cent of all students that business is entitled to make a profit! Seven out of ten students subscribe to the traditional belief that private property is valid.

These feelings do not mean that the students are either blind or self-contradictory. They do mean that student views will not fit into older ideological classifications.

4. Less Polarization

Overall, there is less rather than more polarization among the student body than in the past few years. Students seem less dogmatic in their beliefs on both ends of the political spectrum. Significantly fewer students than in 1970, for example, reject the use of force by police. But on the other hand, there is less opposition than in previous years to creating a mass revolutionary party or to the view that the war in Vietnam is "pure imperialism." Similar examples of agnosticism on political matters abound. Students seem prepared to entertain any proposal—radical or conservative. They have become less ideological. Here, once again, the lessened polarization is probably due not to doctrinal shifts but to a lower level of student involvement in public affairs.

5. Changing Moral Codes

Student views on what is morally right or wrong present some surprising contrasts. More students think it is more immoral to collect welfare when one is capable of working than believe it is morally wrong to pay one's way through college by selling dope. And pilferage—taking things without paying for them—is more widely considered as immoral than destroying private property, selling dope, interchanging partners among couples, and general disregard of the law.

6. Repercussions of Vietnam

The impact of the war in Southeast Asia and its repercussions continue to dominate student thinking. Students say they are more concerned about Vietnam than last year; the war in Vietnam is the No. 1 social issue of greatest concern to students— ahead of pollution and poverty, and it is the No. 1 indication students cite as evidence that things are not working properly in the country. As a result, students are becoming increasingly pacifist in outlook: there is a marked trend toward rejecting wars as instruments of policy for almost any reason—protecting our national interests, preserving positions of power, fighting for honor, protecting allies, keeping commitments, and even counteracting aggression. Only a tiny proportion of students (7%) believe that ending the war in Vietnam will usher in a period of peace. Most of them are concerned that our present policies will inevitably lead to other Vietnams. The importance of patriotism as a personal value has declined over the past several years.

7. Justice

The malfunctioning of our system of justice is one of the major criticisms students level at our society. Those who students feel are assured of a fair trial and due process of the law are: landlords, war criminals, tax evaders, and polluters. Those who a majority feel cannot be assured of a fair trial are: Black Panthers, antiwar leaders, dissenting servicemen, and homosexuals.

8. Effects of the Economy

The softness in the economy has had a measurable effect on the student values. Fewer students this year than in previous years take affluence for granted or think they can make as much money as they wish. Job security and money as career considerations have been significantly upgraded by students this year.

9. Anti-Violence

A massive revulsion against the idea of violence has taken place, but there is more student acceptance than in previous years of tactics verging on overt violence such as blockades, ultimatums, and sit-ins.

10. Marriage

There has been a substantial increase over the past few years in the number of students who believe that marriage is obsolete; and considerable interest exists in living in communes and living off the land.

11. Sex Mores

Major changes in sexual morality have taken place over the past few years, with far wider acceptance today of casual premarital sexual relations, extramarital sexual relations, and homosexuality between consenting adults.

12. Technology

In 1969, the majority of students welcomed the prospect of technological improvement. Today only a minority feel this way.

In the pages that follow, innumerable findings, many of them of great significance, are presented. Compositely, they present a fascinating picture of a culture in transition as mirrored in its college youth. We see students seeking to blend old values with new ones, youthful impulses with adult concerns, and ancient rites of passage with the desire to be free of older traditions and ceremonies. The mirror may be distorted, but the reflection it gives of our society is one of the most valuable we can possess.

The research findings are organized into two major parts. Following a brief chapter on method, Chapters 3 through 6, in Part I, describe the student body as a whole. Chapters 7 through 11, in Part II, present a series of profiles on student subgroups. The 8,000,000 young people in college today are hardly a homogeneous population. They come from a wide variety of family backgrounds, from all parts of the country and from all races, creeds, and religions. There are striking differences to be found within each type of breakdown. In Part II we examine these differences, contrasting New Left students with the more Career-Minded, minority-group students with the majority, men with women, and Democrats and Republicans with students holding no party affiliation.

CHAPTER 2

A Word About Method

OVER THE PAST SEVERAL DECADES, social research reports have grown in importance as sources of news and as guides to those who make public policy. Published research reports range from single-column newspaper accounts of public opinion polls to recent elaborate studies for Presidential commissions on obscenity, the effects of violence on TV, the causes of riots in the cities, campus unrest, drug addiction, and the impact of income maintenance on the work motivations of the poor.

Such studies enjoy a paradoxical fate: the more important they become as influences on public policy, the less well read they may be. This happens for one main reason: the currency of such studies is numbers, and most people don't find wading through masses of numbers an enjoyable reading experience. It is, of course, possible to describe human change, even among large populations, without reference to statistics. Our most gifted historians do it all the time. But in reporting a particular study, or series of related studies as in the present instance, we would lose a great deal in precision if we were to push the statistics into the background or to bury them in an indigestible lump of tables in a technical appendix.

We have opted for a different solution. While it may be impossible to present social research statistics as literature—numbers simply do not lend themselves to as felicitous treatment as, say, case histories or essays—it is possible to present them clearly and simply. Tables reporting survey findings can be read by anyone if they are not cluttered or unduly technical in form. And, by way of compensation, the patterns formed by survey statistics can have an inherent fascination that make up, in part, for their awkwardness as literature.

In assessing the accuracy of any survey there are three things to

13

look at—the sample, the questions asked, and the method of analysis. Thus, in presenting the research findings we have followed a few simple rules in each of these areas.

The Sample

Of the three, the sample—the method of finding a valid cross-section of the population to interview—is by far the most scientific aspect of survey research. By following certain well-accepted procedures of random selection based on probability methods, the amount of possible error due to the sampling method can be calculated with precision. This is the case with this particular study[1] even though sampling issues are relatively more critical in surveys used to predict elections or to calculate shifts in employment rates than in studies which describe attitudes, values, and beliefs. Two or three percentage points may make all the difference in the world in calling an election or discerning an employment trend. But when we examine people's core values we are generally dealing with larger gross differences. For example, over the past few years students have been asked how they feel about the prohibitions against marijuana, heroin, and mind-expanding drugs such as LSD. In 1970, the first year the question was asked about heroin, 86 per cent of all students interviewed said that they easily accepted the prohibition against heroin. In 1971, 83 per cent gave the same response. In our analyses, we ignore that 3 per cent difference which is neither statistically nor substantively significant, waiting until next year to identify a possible trend. We do, however, treat the pattern of student answers to questions on marijuana differently. In 1968, a majority of students (55%) said that they easily accepted the prohibition against marijuana. In 1969, the number had fallen to 48 per cent. In 1970 it remained at 48 per cent. In 1971 it dropped to 42 per cent. In our discussion of findings, we call attention to this pattern for several reasons. First of all, the spread between the 1968 and 1971 figures is substantial—an absolute drop of 13 percentage points and a much larger change in proportion; secondly, we have four consecutive readings all moving in the same direction; and third, these findings are consistent with our other find-

---

[1] See Appendix for details of the sampling plan.

ings about student reactions to comparable forms of social restraints. Our first rule of thumb, therefore, is to look for meaningful differences and ignore small variations even when statistically significant, identify trends where these exist, and search for consistent patterns.

The Questions

When the results of a study on attitudes and values are questionable, the source of the trouble most often lies with the questions asked rather than with the sample design. It is not uncommon to find ultra-sophistication in the methods used to insure that a representative sample will be queried, alongside of naïveté or even lack of objectivity in the questions asked.

In the early days of survey research, the questions were thought up by the researchers themselves without guidance from any source except their own ingenuity and imagination. It gradually became clear, however, that this procedure commonly produced findings which were vague, inconclusive, or all too obvious. As social science research techniques evolved, researchers turned their attention to finding new, empirically rooted sources for their questions. Nowadays, in large-scale surveys designed to explore any subtle or complex topic, the questions asked in the survey generally come either from previous research or from pre-survey studies specially designed to yield hypotheses and salient questions.

This two-step process is basic to the use of survey research as a method for gaining more than superficial insights about large populations of people. When the unit of study is a population—be it the general public or a cross-section of some special public such as business executives, students, physicians, or heart patients—we are faced with the task of reconciling two seemingly incompatible requirements. These are: the need for rigidity in the questioning procedure and the need for flexibility in the interests of obtaining full, rich information from every individual. Everyone who is interviewed in a cross-section sample must be asked the same questions, and the question wording must not change from one respondent to the next or from one year to the next when trends are being measured. When, for example, the study reports that the Democratic Party has lost much ground among students over the past few years, one has the right to expect that the same question on this topic has been posed to comparable cross-sections of students in previous years.

This need for rigidity, however, conflicts with the equally important need to stimulate thoughtful answers to questions that people may not be reflecting upon at the time of the interview. A majority of college students are troubled by the state of our society and almost all of them have theories about what is wrong and why things are not working properly. But one student is facile and articulate, swamping the interviewer with a long inventory of the country's ills while another student who feels just as deeply is not able to express himself as clearly or easily. How, then, is it possible to reconcile the need for a rigid order of similarly phrased questions with the need for exploration in depth of the full range of an individual's beliefs, attitudes, and values? Here is where a two-step approach proves its value. In the pre-survey step, free-form discussions are held with individuals or small groups of eight to ten people at a time. In these sessions, flexibility is the rule; there is no set order to the questions, their wording varies from interview to interview, there is extensive probing and challenging by the interviewer and the person interviewed is encouraged to speak about his thoughts and beliefs in any way he wishes. The great flexibility of these free-form interviews produces much of the raw material that will later be organized into the more rigid structure of the formal survey and permits the asking of questions within the student's frame of reference rather than imposing the researcher's own frame of reference on him. And they suggest many new questions the researcher had not thought of asking.

To illustrate: in the pre-survey phase of the 1971 study we asked students, in group and individual interviews, to contrast their present mood with how they felt last spring. (The spring of 1970, the reader will recall, was the time of Cambodia, Kent, and Jackson State, a period of crisis and tension on American campuses.) Out of these discussions we identified twenty changes of mood that were spontaneously brought up by the students interviewed. Some students said they were now more radical than last year; others said they were more conservative. Some said they were more serious about studying, others said they were less serious. Still others reported that they were angrier or more discouraged or more fearful about getting a job in the future or more alienated from the society than they were last spring.

The point at issue is that these mood changes were not dreamed up by some middle-aged researcher sitting at a Manhattan desk. The question of determining how typical or representative or widespread they were would then become the main task of the formal survey with all of its cumbersome apparatus of randomized selection of colleges and students, rigidly structured interviews, coding and tabulating procedures, and computer-based data processing programs.

Here, then, are the rules of thumb adhered to in asking and reporting on student answers to questions:

1. Only ask questions about student values and attitudes which are based on empirical sources—either previous studies or special pre-survey interviews and discussions;
2. Provide the reader with the exact wording of each question, and
3. Indicate those few instances where wording changes in trend questions were introduced and state what they are.

Analysis

A final word about the methods of analysis used in these studies. In recent years, the mathematical techniques for analyzing survey data have greatly increased in power, subtlety, and sophistication. They have also, however, increased in the level of statistical understanding required of the reader. Since the purpose of this book is to make the findings and the basis for them accessible to all interested readers, we have used methods of analysis which presuppose no technical background. Thus, we have chosen to adhere to the most straightforward method of analysis available to us, that of simple comparisons between subgroups of students or between cross-sections of college students interviewed in different years.

The book contains many tables. With a few exceptions, each table has been stripped to its essentials. The text also includes key statistics selected from the tables, so that the reader who wishes to skip the tables may do so. Though many of the findings are cited in the text the tables do, of course, contain a great many additional findings. Scanning the tables also permits the reader to form his own interpretation as to meaning. Except for the personal commentary by Daniel Yankelovich, which is Part III of the book under the title "The New

Naturalism," interpretations by the researchers have been kept to a practical minimum. The act of interpretation is, however, inherent in the very act of writing and selecting. And so the reader will recognize that some interpretation has inevitably crept into the text.

CHAPTER 3

The Changing Student Mood

THE SETTING FOR THIS STUDY is the prevailing student mood in the spring of 1971—a mood which is both complex yet perceptibly clear.

Its essence is the strange combination of present happiness with concern about the future and a curious blending of private contentment and public despair. It contains little anger or hate—but deep underlying skepticism about the society in which we live, and many doubts about its ability to cope with inequalities, injustices, and social problems. The violent student reactions of previous years have given way to privatism, to the search for a more satisfactory life style, and to new values and mores.

These findings run through the responses to two questions asked of the students about their present mood and how it compares with their own feelings of a year or two ago.

In one of the first questions in the interview, students were asked to choose from among a wide variety of phrases those that best described their present mood.[1] The two top-rated choices—and the only ones selected by a majority of the students—were: confused about the future (55%) and happy (50%). At the other extreme, the phrases selected by the fewest students were angry (8%) and full of hate and violence (2%).

In between these two extremes were phrases such as optimistic about the future (34%); worried (31%); skeptical (30%); quiet (20%); and bored (17%).

Confused about the future, happy, somewhat optimistic but quiet and perhaps a little bored: in capsule form, these phrases capture the essence of a mood that contrasts sharply with the Cambodia, Kent-

---

[1] See Table 1 for the full list of responses.

Jackson period with its atmosphere of grim tenseness shot through with violence, anger, and anxiety.

Student Recognition of Changes of Mood

The students themselves recognize the difference the year has made both in their own mood and that of the campus community as a whole. The two dimensions of student mood we investigated most thoroughly were the private/personal sphere and the political sphere.

Of the two, the private/personal components of mood change are the most clear-cut. In answer to a question in which students were asked to contrast their present mood with how they felt in the previous spring, the widest mood shift, as seen in retrospect by the students interviewed, was an increased involvement in their own private life and concerns (see Table 2). Sixty-one per cent of the students said that they were more involved in their own private life now than in the previous year, 12 per cent reported less involvement in personal matters and the other 27 per cent said their mood had not changed. The net difference between those more and those less self-involved is a huge 49 per cent—the single largest mood change uncovered by the research. Other large-scale mood shifts were: students reporting that they are happier now than the year before (40% net difference), more serious about studying (24% net difference), more fearful about being able to get a job in the future (28% net difference).

The shift of student mood on the social/political front is considerably more ambiguous. On the one hand, students describe themselves as less violence-prone and less alienated, and they see student radicalism as diminishing. On the other hand, they see themselves personally as growing less conservative and more radical. They say they are now more skeptical about the truthfulness of our government leaders, less confident about the underlying health of the country and more concerned about Vietnam. At the same time, they tend to be discouraged about their ability to bring about desired changes and are less willing to participate in protests.

Small wonder, perhaps, that they feel confused. What we are seeing is the consequence of a shift of emotions away from public affairs to private affairs. The doubts, the misgivings, the skepticism about public affairs are still present, but the intensity of the impetus toward activism appears to be waning.

More specifically, the findings show these patterns:[2]

—Two-thirds of all students in 1970 thought that student radicalism would continue to grow. In 1971 the figure is cut in half and only one-third think that campus radicalism is growing.

—A majority of students (52%) say they are more skeptical of the truthfulness of our government leaders than they were the year before.

—On balance, students feel growing doubts about the nation's state of health. Forty-two per cent say they are less confident about our country's underlying health than they were the year before, in contrast to half that number (20%) who say they are more confident.

—Forty-four per cent of the students say they are less accepting of violence as a legitimate tactic to achieve desired social change than they were the year before. Only 12 per cent say that they now favor violence more than they did previously.

—Four out of ten (41%) claim to be less conservative in their political thinking today than the year before, in contrast to only 14 per cent who claim to be more conservative. Twenty-seven per cent of the students say they are more radical in their political thinking than they were the year before.

—Twice as many students report being less alienated than they were the year before (33% to 17%).

These findings are our first indication of many we shall see as the narrative unfolds that the student body as a whole appears to be less politicized than it was in the previous year. To be politicized means not merely to hold certain political attitudes. It also means to live, act, feel, and be in a political mode. And students today have unmistakably withdrawn a considerable amount of their feeling and being from the political domain into the domain of the private and the personal. Whether one agrees or disagrees with this shift of mood, whether one welcomes it with relief or deplores it, whether it is temporary or long lasting, the facts at present show that students continue to be upset

---

[2] Findings are based on Tables 1–4 at the end of this chapter.

and mistrustful about the state of the nation but they are paying less emotional heed to social/political events, and more attention to private affairs. They also seem to be more content and less depressed and off-balance.

Table **1.**   Phrases Which Best Describe Current Student Mood*
(Also see page 215)

	Total Students 1971**
	%
Confused about the future	►55
Happy	►50
Optimistic about the future	34
Worried	31
Skeptical	30
Encouraged	28
Involved	28
Frustrated	27
Satisfied	24
Stimulated	23
Serene	22
Weary	22
Disgusted	22
Discouraged	21
Quiet	20
Bored	17
Depressed	17
Apathetic	17
Cynical	15
Agitated	13
Withdrawn	11
Angry	8
Full of hate and violence	2
Not sure	11
None	2

* **Question 1c:** "Which of these phrases best describes your own current mood and state of mind?"
** Asked only in 1971.

Table 2. Students Contrast Their Present Mood with How They Felt Last Year* *(Also see page 216)*

	Total Students 1971**			
	More	Less	Same	Net Difference More/Less
	%	%	%	%
Involved in your own private life and concerns	61	12	27	►+49
Concerned about what is happening in Vietnam	57	11	32	►+46
Happy in your own personal life	55	15	30	►+40
Skeptical of the truthfulness of government leaders	52	15	33	►+37
Fearful about being able to get a job in the future	50	22	28	►+28
Serious about studying	48	24	28	►+24
Confident about which tactics are right and effective in achieving change	36	21	43	+15
Close to your family	36	18	46	+18
Involved in working for change	32	17	51	+15
Discouraged about the chances for bringing about desired changes in the society	30	22	48	+8
Fearful of repression	29	19	52	+10
Convinced about the impotence and powerlessness of individuals like yourself to effect change	29	28	43	+1
Angry and determined to do something	27	19	54	+8
Radical in your political thinking	27	17	56	+10
Interested in working in a political campaign	25	28	47	−3
Willing to participate in protests	22	28	50	−6
Confident about the underlying health of the country	20	42	38	►−22
Alienated from the society	17	33	50	►−16
Conservative in your political thinking	14	41	45	►−27
Accepting of violence as a legitimate tactic to achieve desired social change	12	44	44	►−32

* **Question 1d:** "I'd like to ask you to contrast your present mood with how you felt last spring. For example, are you more [READ LIST] now than you were last year, less, or about the same?"
** Asked only in 1971.

THE COLLEGE SCENE

Table 3. Contrast of Student Reaction to Invasion of Laos vs. Cambodia*

	Total Students 1971**
	%
Student opposition to Laos less vigorous	
True	►67
Not true	7
Not sure	26

* **Question 3b:** "Some people have felt that student opposition to the invasion of Laos was considerably less vigorous and vocal than to the Cambodia invasion a year ago. Has this been true around here?"
** Asked only in 1971.

Table 4. Student Views About Whether Campus Radicalism Is Growing or Declining*
(Also see page 217)

	Total Students	
	1971	1970**
	%	%
Student radicalism		
Continuing to grow	34	►67
Leveling off	►43	30
Declining	12	3
Not sure	11	—

* **Question 17a:** "Do you feel that student radicalism is continuing to grow, leveling off, or declining?"
** Asked only in 1971 and 1970.

CHAPTER 4

Personal and Social Values

LET US TURN NOW from student mood to the changes in social and personal values that have taken place over the past five years. Mood, by definition, is a transitory state of mind assuming one coloration today, another tomorrow. In this chapter and the next two, we turn to a more enduring phenomenon—the emergence of new and changing values so sweeping in character that, at least in their extreme forms, they merit the label "revolution."

The counterculture is no longer unfamiliar. The media have played up every aberration of dress, every new expression of mysticism, every variation of communal living style, every sex experiment, every Yippie-Hippie-rip-off-tear-down-pull-up adventure of the counterculture it can flush out.

The task of social research is almost the opposite of that assumed by the media. Two opposing concepts of "news" are at issue. Social research is the study of the typical, not of the flamboyant, the freakish, and the colorful. And, from the point of view of what is typical on campus today, there is a real "values" revolution unfolding.

Truly it is not as extreme in form as the counterculture. But it may be more significant for the future of the country since it is affecting a broad cross-section of young people rather than a small minority.

The main themes of the New Values, as the research reveals them, are:

—Challenge to authority.
—The search for substitutes for traditional religious values, particularly those that reflect the "Puritan Ethic."
—A new sexual morality.
—A questioning of wars as instruments of policy and of patriotism itself.

25

—A search for cooperant rather than competitive life styles.

—Dissatisfaction with marriage in its traditional form of a one-family house and two children.

—A shifting from the extrinsic rewards of career (money and status) to its inherent satisfactions.

—A change of emphasis from achievement via hard work to living in closer harmony with one's peers and with nature itself.

Students are struggling to adapt these New Values to older traditional life styles, creating in the process a phase of experimentation and transition that is sometimes exhilarating, sometimes painful, and often incomprehensible. But always the search goes on, pursued with great intensity. Year by year it reaches ever more deeply the great mass of students.

In this chapter we shall be looking at these New Values which we have grouped together as cultural values in contrast to the political values we will be examining in the next chapter.

These New Values are discussed under the following headings:

1. Wars worth fighting
2. Challenge to authority
3. Morals and the Puritan Ethic
4. Personal values
5. Marriage
6. Career

Wars Worth Fighting

Even in the brief time span between 1968 and 1971, student attitudes toward war as an instrument of policy or an expression of patriotism or moral values have changed dramatically. Year by year there has been a consistent erosion in the willingness of students to fight wars for any reason. Indeed, in 1971 there was only one objective which even 50 per cent of the students saw as justifying going to war —counteracting aggression. And even in this case, there was a considerable decline from the original 64 per cent reading when the question was first asked in 1968.

Over the almost five-year period, when students were asked to indi-

26

cate under what circumstances they felt a war was worth fighting, the results were as follows:

—Protecting our national interests: supported by a majority of students in 1968 (54%); down to 39 per cent in 1969; 31 per cent in 1970 and 30 per cent in 1971.

—Containing Communists: seen as worthwhile by 45 per cent of the students in 1968, 43 per cent in 1969; 32 per cent in 1970 and 29 per cent in 1971; or a total falloff of a third in a period of slightly less than five years.

—Maintaining our position of power in the world: 35 per cent in 1968 to 19 per cent in 1971.

—Preserving our honor: 33 per cent in 1968, 18 per cent in 1971.

A similar, though less dramatic, pattern can be seen in the results on the worthwhileness of fighting wars to protect allies, counteracting aggression and keeping a commitment.

The detailed findings on this question are well worth careful study. They are shown in Table 5 at the end of this chapter.

Challenge to Authority

One of the hallmarks of the campus cultural revolution is youthful resistance to an automatic acceptance of authority, whatever form the authority takes, be it laws, police, bosses, or conventional hair styles.

Here are some of the specific manifestations of this increasing resistance to authority:

—In 1968, six out of ten students (59%) found that they could easily accept the power and authority of the police. In 1971, that number had been reduced to 45 per cent.

—Accepting prohibition against marijuana, as we indicated earlier, has also proved to be an increasingly difficult restraint, dropping from a 55 per cent level of "easy acceptance" in 1968 to 42 per cent in 1971.

—Resistance to other restraints follows a similar pattern. Many fewer students than formerly find it easy to accept outward conformity for the sake of career advancement or to abide by laws with which they do not agree.

—The greatest single erosion of relations to authority is in the "boss" relationship and the work situation. In 1968, over half of all students (56%) did not mind the future prospect of being bossed around on the job. This number fell to 49 per cent in 1969, 43 per cent in 1970 and down to 36 per cent in 1971. The result: today two out of three students do not easily see themselves submitting to the authority of the "boss."

—A student's relation to authority of all kinds—including the "boss" —is at best one of grudging but not easy acceptance.

There is only one restraint which a majority of students reject outright—keeping their views to themselves. It is this factor, perhaps, which tends to becloud the fact that other restraints are accepted— even if reluctantly.

Current restraints most students accept easily are: the prohibitions against heroin (83%), LSD and other mind-expanding drugs (66%). Those which the fewest students find it easy to accept are conformity for the sake of career advancement (15%) and abiding by laws one doesn't agree with (13%).[1]

Morals and the Puritan Ethic

There is nothing that defines a culture more sharply than its moral code—the activities it labels as morally acceptable or wrong. The 1971 study reveals a picture of morals in transition, a curious blend of the traditional and the new. The findings show that on campus many tenets of the traditional Puritan Ethic are changing and none more so than values relating to sexual morality.

A majority of students (56%) want still more acceptance of sexual freedom—a substantial increase from the 43 per cent figure in 1969.

What sexual freedom means is clearly indicated by student response to other questions on the subject. Only one out of four now regard casual premarital sex relations as morally wrong (down from 34% in

---

[1] See Table 6 for detailed findings.

1969), or condemn relations between consenting homosexuals as immoral (down even more sharply from 42%), or reject on moral grounds the having of an abortion.

Moral reservations do increase when marriage enters the picture. But here, too, the climate is changing. Only four out of ten students (42%) believe it is immoral to plan and have children outside of marriage. Six out of ten (57%) regard extramarital sex relations as morally wrong (down from 77% in 1969). An equal number (59%) condemn interchanging partners among couples. It is interesting to contrast these views on sexual morality with other widely held moral beliefs of the students.

The most universal of the traditional moral beliefs held on campus, significant in the light of so much talk about the generation gap, is that "children should respect their parents" (87%). At an equally high level is the belief that "society needs some legally based authority in order to prevent chaos" (86%).

A majority of students also believe that it is morally wrong "to take things without paying for them" (78%), "to collect welfare when you can work" (75%), "to destroy private property" (72%) and "to pay one's way through college by selling dope" (63%).

Other values associated with the Puritan Ethic investigated in this study included savings, duty, belief in control over one's destiny, religion, and work. Here are some of the relevant findings:

Control Over One's Destiny

One traditional belief, indeed perhaps the only one, that has actually registered even a slight gain in acceptance among students is the idea that a person's strength of character has a great deal to do with his ability to control his destiny. In 1968, a bare majority (51%) subscribed to this concept. It is now held by six out of ten students (60%)—a relatively small gain but a significant one since it runs counter to the general trend.

Saving

Two-thirds of the students hold the traditional view that everyone should save as much money as he can to avoid depending on family and friends; still a solid number—but down from the high 76 per cent figure in 1969.

Organized Religion

Two-thirds of all students reject organized religion as an important value in a person's life, an increase of 7 percentage points since the question was last asked in 1969. Belief in organized religion has similarly declined from 38 per cent that year to the current reading of 31 per cent on "religion is a very important value in one's life."

Work

Students, by and large, no longer subscribe to the traditional view that hard work will pay off. Nor do they regard work as an important value. Yet in spite of these feelings, there is no visible sign of any increased tendency toward avoiding hard work as a necessary part of life.

The erosion in the traditional belief that "hard work will always pay off" represents as vast a shift of values as those taking place even with regard to sexual morality.

—In 1968, seven out of ten students (69%) held to this belief; by 1969, this number was reduced to 56 per cent—but still a majority. But in 1971 only four out of ten (39%) held the view that hard work is sure to pay off.
—Furthermore, work does not rank particularly high as an important value in the students' lives, falling far below the emphasis placed on love, friendship, education, self-expression, family, and privacy.

Yet both of these student attitudes on work must be examined and understood in the context of the finding that no increase has occurred in the desire to work hard. More than four years ago in 1968, only 31 per cent of the students said they would welcome less emphasis on working hard. This figure still holds at 30 per cent.

We may sum up this discussion on traditional morality by citing one general finding: several years ago, not even a majority of students felt that it was very important to live a "clean moral life" (45%). In 1971, one-third (34%) shared this conviction.

Personal Values

The personal values most universally endorsed by students are those of love and friendship. These values are cited by nine out of ten students (87%) as very important values in their personal life. Moreover, strong allegiance to the ideals of love and friendship has not changed over the past few years.

Other values held to be very important by a majority of students are: education (74%), "expressing your opinion" (74%), family (65%), privacy (64%), doing things for others (59%), and being creative (52%). Very little change has occurred in the patterning of those values considered most important since the last measurement in 1969. At the other extreme, the lowest-ranked values are religion (31%), patriotism (27%), beauty (19%), and money (18%).

It is especially interesting to note how low students value "not compromising one's beliefs" (35%) and "changing society" (34%) in the hierarchy of values. In the past few years the impression has been created that changing society, combating hypocrisy, and living rigidly by one's beliefs were virtually universal characteristics of today's college students. Yet, these values rank highly for just one-third of the student body, and they are far less general in their appeal than values with more personal emotional roots such as the desire for friendship, for expressing one's opinion, for privacy, for doing things for others, for family, and for being close to nature.

For the past several years students have been asked what value changes they would most welcome. Prior to 1971, the leading changes they desired were: more emphasis on self-expression, less emphasis on money, more emphasis on law and order, technological improvement, and sexual freedom. In 1971, the hierarchy shifted somewhat. Greater emphasis on self-expression and less emphasis on money still lead the list. But now law and order is down, sexual freedom is up, and technological improvement is way down.

Marriage

Student values on the subject of marriage and family can be summarized in two statements. First: there is an approximately 70/30 split in the student population, with the majority pro-marriage, and the minority either anti-marriage or not sure. Second: family and children are somewhat more important than marriage.

Specifically, the key findings on marriage are these:

—The number of students who believe that marriage is obsolete has increased substantially—from 24 per cent in 1969 to 34 per cent in 1971.
—Most students look forward to being married; three out of ten do not or are not sure about it.
—Eight out of ten students say they are interested in having children; only one out of ten is not. The balance are not sure how they feel.
—Almost four out of ten students are interested in living in a commune (36%)—most of them for a short time, but some of them permanently.
—An even larger number of students is interested in living off the land. Here again the pattern is the same. More than four out of ten (43%) would like to try living off the land—most of them for a year or two but some would like to settle permanently in a small agricultural and rural area with other young people.

Career

Student values associated with career choice are also sharply defined:

—Four out of five students (79%) hold the belief that commitment to a meaningful career is a very important part of a person's life, making this one of the most universally held beliefs.
—The number of students who attend college primarily for career purposes has slowly but steadily increased since the fall of 1967, and correspondingly, the proportion of students who take the career benefits of college for granted has decreased. In the study

32

reported in 1968, 55 per cent of all students classified themselves as interested in college mainly for career-related benefits. In 1969, the number was 57 per cent, in 1970 it was 60 per cent, and this year it is 61 per cent. These changes are nowhere near as great as other changes cited in the report but they do seem to form a pattern.

—Students rank "the opportunity to make a contribution," "job challenge," and "ability to find self-expression" at the top of the list of influences on their career choice. Job prestige is ranked at the bottom. This pattern has held remarkably constant over the past four studies. The major changes in ranking of influences on career choice relate to the role of money and job security. These have increased substantially in importance over last year (and moderately over preceding years).

—For the past three years students were asked two questions to gauge how much they take their money-earning ability and success for granted. One question is: "Do you have any doubts about making as much money as you may want to—whatever the amount is?" The other question is: "Do you have any doubts about your ability to become successful—as you define success?" It is perhaps significant that no change has occurred in the pattern of answers to the second question about success, but a substantial change has taken place with respect to self-doubts about making money. In the 1969 and 1970 studies, six out of ten students said they had no doubts about their ability to make as much money as they might want to. In 1971 the number fell to 50 per cent.

—Finally, the major barrier students see standing in the way of securing desirable work is their attitude toward authority. No obstacle comes even close to this one, including political views, style of dress or unwillingness to conform.

Detailed findings on social and personal values, marriage and career are to be found in the tables which follow.

Table 5. Values Worth Fighting a War for*
(Also see page 218)

	Total Students			
	1971	1970	1969	1968
	%	%	%	%
Counteracting aggression				
Worth fighting for	50	50	56	64
Not worth fighting for	12	8	6	5
Depends on circumstances	38	42	38	31
Protecting allies				
Worth fighting for	31	28	38	44
Not worth fighting for	17	12	12	12
Depends on circumstances	52	60	50	44
Protecting our national interests				
Worth fighting for	►30	►31	►39	►54
Not worth fighting for	19	16	14	10
Depends on circumstances	51	53	47	36
Containing the Communists				
Worth fighting for	►29	►32	►43	►45
Not worth fighting for	32	30	25	25
Depends on circumstances	39	38	32	30
Maintaining our position of power in the world				
Worth fighting for	►19	►17	►25	►35
Not worth fighting for	45	49	39	35
Depends on circumstances	36	34	36	30
Fighting for our honor				
Worth fighting for	►18	►17	►25	►33
Not worth fighting for	44	47	38	32
Depends on circumstances	38	36	37	35
Keeping a commitment				
Worth fighting for	14	14	14	20
Not worth fighting for	24	20	20	18
Depends on circumstances	62	66	66	62

* **Question 9b:** "Which of these do you believe are worth fighting a war for, which do you believe are not worth fighting a war for, which do you believe it depends on the special circumstances?"

Table 6. Acceptance of Social Restraints*
(Also see page 219)

	Total Students			
	1971	1970	1969	1968
	%	%	%	%
Prohibition against heroin*				
Accept easily	83	86	—	—
Accept reluctantly	7	7	—	—
Reject outright	10	7	—	—
Prohibition against LSD (mind-expansion drugs)†				
Accept easily	66	78	73	—
Accept reluctantly	16	10	11	—
Reject outright	18	16	16	—
Power and authority of the police				
Accept easily	▶45	▶45	▶48	▶59
Accept reluctantly	40	45	42	30
Reject outright	15	10	10	11
Prohibition against marijuana				
Accept easily	▶42	▶48	▶48	▶55
Accept reluctantly	22	22	20	15
Reject outright	36	30	32	30
Power and authority of the "boss" in a work situation				
Accept easily	▶36	▶43	▶49	▶56
Accept reluctantly	48	50	45	37
Reject outright	16	7	6	7
Conforming in matters of clothing and personal grooming				
Accept easily	33	39	33	37
Accept reluctantly	34	31	29	25
Reject outright	33	30	38	38

(Continued on next page)

* **Question 16:** "To be even more specific, which of the following restraints imposed by society and its institutions do you accept easily, which do you accept reluctantly and which do you reject outright?"

** Asked only in 1971 and 1970.

† Not asked in 1968. Asked about "LSD" in 1969 and 1970. Asked about "mind-expansion drugs" in 1971.

	Total Students			
	1971	1970	1969	1968
	%	%	%	%
Settling down to a routine‡				
Accept easily	26	—	—	—
Accept reluctantly	40	—	—	—
Reject outright	34	—	—	—
Living like everyone else				
Accept easily	25	—	—	—
Accept reluctantly	33	—	—	—
Reject outright	42	—	—	—
Keep views to self‡				
Accept easily	16	—	—	—
Accept reluctantly	32	—	—	—
Reject outright	52	—	—	—
Outward conformity for the sake of career advancement				
Accept easily	▶15	▶11	▶14	▶29
Accept reluctantly	46	53	47	36
Reject outright	39	36	39	35
Abiding by laws you don't agree with				
Accept easily	▶13	▶17	▶15	▶29
Accept reluctantly	67	66	71	57
Reject outright	20	17	14	14

‡ Asked only in 1971.

Table 7.   Activities Seen as Morally Wrong*
(Also see page 220)

	Total Students	
	1971	1969**
	%	%
Activities morally wrong		
Taking things without paying for them†	78	—
Collecting welfare when you could work†	75	—
Destroying private property†	72	—
Paying one's way through college by selling dope†	63	—
Interchanging partners among couples†	59	—
Breaking the law†	57	—
Extramarital sexual relations	►57	►77
Planning and having children without formal marriage† ..	42	—
Leaving the country to avoid the draft†	28	—
Having an abortion	27	36
Relations between consenting homosexuals	►26	►42
Casual premarital sexual relations	25	34

* **Question 12a:** "Which of the following activities do you feel are morally wrong from your personal point of view?"
** Asked only in 1971 and 1969.
† Asked only in 1971.

Table 8.   Values Important in One's Life*
(Also see page 221)

	Total Students	
	1971	1969**
	%	%
Love		
Very important	87	85
Fairly important	12	14
Not very important	1	1

(Continued on next page)

* **Question 10b:** "What role does each of the following play in your life—is it very important to you, fairly important, or not very important to you?"
** Asked only in 1971 and 1969.

	Total Students	
	1971	1969**
	%	%
Friendship		
Very important	87	85
Fairly important	12	14
Not very important	1	1
Education		
Very important	74	80
Fairly important	24	19
Not very important	2	1
Expressing your opinion†		
Very important	74	—
Fairly important	24	—
Not very important	2	—
Family†		
Very important	65	—
Fairly important	30	—
Not very important	5	—
Privacy		
Very important	64	61
Fairly important	31	34
Not very important	5	5
Doing things for others		
Very important	59	51
Fairly important	39	43
Not very important	2	6
Being creative†		
Very important	52	—
Fairly important	38	—
Not very important	10	—
Being close to nature†		
Very important	47	—
Fairly important	40	—
Not very important	13	—

(Continued on next page)

† Asked only in 1971.

PERSONAL AND SOCIAL VALUES

	Total Students	
	1971	1969**
	%	%
Work†		
Very important	45	—
Fairly important	46	—
Not very important	9	—
Comfort†		
Very important	40	—
Fairly important	49	—
Not very important	11	—
Not compromising belief†		
Very important	35	—
Fairly important	46	—
Not very important	19	—
Changing society		
Very important	34	33
Fairly important	50	46
Not very important	16	21
Living a clean, moral life		
Very important	►34	►45
Fairly important	42	37
Not very important	24	18
Religion		
Very important	31	38
Fairly important	33	31
Not very important	36	31
Patriotism		
Very important	27	35
Fairly important	38	42
Not very important	►35	►23
Beauty†		
Very important	19	—
Fairly important	52	—
Not very important	29	—
Money		
Very important	18	18
Fairly important	59	65
Not very important	23	17

Table 9.   Extent of Belief in Traditional Values*
(Also see pages 222–223)

	Total Students		
	1971	1969	1968**
	%	%	%
Children should respect their parents†			
Believe	87	—	—
Don't believe	13	—	—
Society needs some legally based authority in order to prevent chaos‡			
Believe	86	92	—
Don't believe	14	8	—
Business is entitled to make a profit†			
Believe	85	—	—
Don't believe	15	—	—
Commitment to a meaningful career is a very important part of a person's life†			
Believe	79	—	—
Don't believe	21	—	—
Anyone who violates the law for reasons of conscience should be willing to accept the legal consequences†			
Believe	70	—	—
Don't believe	30	—	—
The right to private property is sacred‡			
Believe	69	75	—
Don't believe	31	25	—
Everyone should save as much money as he can and not have to lean on family and friends the minute he runs into financial problems‡			
Believe	67	76	—
Don't believe	33	24	—

(Continued on next page)

* **Question 11:** "Now I'm going to read you a list of statements which represent some traditional American values. I'd like you to tell me for each one whether you believe or don't believe in it."
** Not asked in 1970.
† Asked only in 1971.
‡ Asked only in 1971 and 1969.

	Total Students		
	1971	1969	1968**
	%	%	%
Duty before pleasure†			
Believe	63	—	—
Don't believe	37	—	—
Competition encourages excellence‡			
Believe	62	72	—
Don't believe	38	28	—
Depending on how much strength and character a person has he can pretty well control what happens to him			
Believe	60	62	51
Don't believe	40	38	49
Hard work will always pay off			
Believe	►39	►56	►69
Don't believe	61	43	31
Belonging to some organized religion is important in a person's life‡			
Believe	35	42	—
Don't believe	65	58	—

THE COLLEGE SCENE

Table **10.**   Value Changes Students Would Welcome*

	Total Students		
	1971	1969	1968**
	%	%	%
More emphasis on self-expression			
Would welcome	80	84	78
Would reject	2	3	3
Leaves indifferent	17	13	19
Don't know	1	—	—
Less emphasis on money			
Would welcome	76	73	65
Would reject	5	10	10
Leaves indifferent	19	17	25
Don't know	—	—	—
More acceptance of sexual freedom†			
Would welcome	►56	►43	—
Would reject	13	24	—
Leaves indifferent	31	33	—
Don't know	—	—	—
More emphasis on law and order			
Would welcome	50	56	60
Would reject	29	25	25
Leaves indifferent	20	19	15
Don't know	1	—	—
More emphasis on technological improvements†			
Would welcome	►39	►56	—
Would reject	20	10	—
Leaves indifferent	40	33	—
Don't know	1	1	—

(Continued on next page)

---

* **Question 10a:** "Many people feel we are undergoing a period of rapid social change in this country and that people's values are changing at the same time. Which of the following changes would you welcome, which would you reject and which would leave you indifferent?"
** Not asked in 1970.
† Not asked in 1968.

42

	Total Students		
	1971	1969	1968**
	%	%	%
Less difference between the sexes‡			
Would welcome	34	—	—
Would reject	35	—	—
Leaves indifferent	31	—	—
Don't know	—	—	—
Less emphasis on working hard			
Would welcome	30	24	31
Would reject	44	48	41
Leaves indifferent	26	28	28
Don't know	—	—	—
More emphasis on ethnic identification‡			
Would welcome	27	—	—
Would reject	39	—	—
Leaves indifferent	34	—	—
Don't know	—	—	—

‡ Asked only in 1971.

Table 11.   Is Marriage Obsolete?*
(Also see page 224)

	Total Students		
	1971	1970	1969**
	%	%	%
Marriage is obsolete			
Agree	►34	►28	►24
Disagree	66	70	76
Not sure	—	2	—

* **Question 12b:** "Some people have said that the present institution of marriage is becoming obsolete. Do you agree or disagree?"
** Not asked in 1968.

43

Table 12.   Does the Traditional Family Structure Work?*

	Total Students 1971** %
Traditional family structure no longer works	
Agree	12
Disagree	►71
Not sure	17

* **Question 13a:** "How do you feel about the criticism that the traditional family structure of mother, father and children living under one roof no longer works?"
** Asked only in 1971.

Table 13.   Looking Forward to Being Married?*

	Total Students 1971** %
Look forward to being married	►61
Don't look forward to being married	14
Already married	7
Don't know	18

* **Question 13b:** "Do you look forward to the idea of being legally married?"
** Asked only in 1971.

Table 14.   Interest in Having Children*

	Total Students 1971** %
Interested in having children	►79
Not interested in having children	9
Not sure	12

* **Question 13c:** "Are you interested in having children?"
** Asked only in 1971.

Table 15.   Interest in Living in Collectives and Communes*
(Also see page 225)

	Total Students 1971**
	%
Interested in living in commune	
Short-term	31 ⎫ 36
Permanent	5 ⎭
Not at all	51
Not sure	13

* **Question 13d:** "Many young people today are living in collectives or communes. Is this something that would interest you on a short-term commitment, such as a few years, on a permanent commitment or not at all?"
** Asked only in 1971.

Table 16.   Interest in Living Off the Land*
(Also see page 225)

	Total Students 1971**
	%
Interested in living off land	
A year or two	34 ⎫ 43
Permanently	9 ⎭
No appeal	44
Not sure	13

* **Question 13e:** "One hears more and more about groups of young people going off to live off the land and settling in small agricultural and rural areas. Is this something that would interest you for a year or two, permanently, or doesn't the idea have appeal for you at all?"
** Asked only in 1971.

Table 17. Career-Minded Students and Those Who Take Affluence for Granted*
(Also see page 226)

	Total Students			
	1971	1970	1969	1968
	%	%	%	%
Career-Minded				
For me, college is mainly a practical matter. With a college education I can earn more money, have a more interesting career and enjoy a better position in the society	61	60	57	55
Take-Affluence-for-Granted**				
I'm not really concerned with the practical benefits of college. I suppose I take them for granted. College for me means something more intangible; perhaps the opportunity to change things rather than make out well within the existing system	►39	►40	►43	►45

* **Question T:** "Here are two statements made by college students on their reasons for going to college. Please indicate which statement comes closest to your own views—even if neither of them fits exactly."
** Called "Forerunners" in previous studies.

Table **18.** Self-Doubts About Making Money and Being Successful*
(Also see page 227)

	Total Students		
	1971	1970	1969**
	%	%	%
Have self-doubts about making money			
Yes	►50	►38	►40
No	50	62	60
Have doubts about being successful†			
Yes	36	—	33
No	64	—	67

* **Question 15b:** "Do you have any doubts about being able to make as much money as you may want to—whatever the amount is?"
  Question 15c: "Do you have any doubts about your ability to be successful as you define success?"
** Not asked in 1968.
† Asked only in 1971 and 1969.

Table **19.** Influences on Career Choice*
(Also see page 228)

	Total Students			
	1971	1970	1969	1968
	%	%	%	%
Chance to make a contribution	70	73	76	75
Challenge of job	66	64	71	76
Ability to express yourself	63	56	66	69
Free time for outside interests**	59	—	—	—
Opportunity to work with other people rather than manipulate them**	59	—	—	—
Security of job†	►46	►33	42	—
Money you earn	►44	►36	41	41
Chance to get ahead**	35	—	—	—
Family	35	41	31	37
Job prestige	22	15	23	24
Other	2	—	—	—

* **Question 15a:** "Which of the considerations on this card will have a relatively strong influence on your choice of career?"
** Asked only in 1971.
† Not asked in 1968.

Table 20. Barriers Toward Getting Work*
(Also see page 229)

	Total Students 1971**
	%
Your attitude toward authority	►25
Your unwillingness to conform	24
Your educational background	17
Your sex	16
Your political views	15
Your style of dress	13
Your race	11
Your family background	6
Your religion	5
None of these	41

* **Question 15d:** "Which of the following do you think could be barriers toward getting the kind of work you want?"
** Asked only in 1971.

CHAPTER 5

Political Values and Ideologies

THE CAMPUS MAY BE the crucible of an emerging social revolution, but it is politics that make headlines. The vast changes in sexual morality, marriage, the relation to money, the work ethic, and the changing relationship to authority—all facets of the social revolution—are the enduring legacy of campus change. Yet, over the past few years, it has been the political side—the strikes, the sit-ins, the bombings, and the protests—that have most disquieted the public.

In the light of the research, the political values of students show themselves to be more volatile than their social values—more subject to swings in both directions, more inconsistent, less thoughtful, and less thoroughly examined. This is not so at the far Left and far Right ends of the political spectrum, but it is for the majority. And the political views of the majority are what counts. It is true that the massive waves of campus unrest of the past few years were created by small numbers of activists. But activists have always been present on campus, as they have in every other domain of American life—in small numbers. It was the support of the mass of students that made the strikes and sit-ins possible and effective. If student protest has now ebbed, we shall not find any great decrease in the number of those who identify themselves with the New Left or other activist groups. Rather, we shall find that the mainstream of student opinion has shifted direction; a shift that is complex and confusing, but nonetheless decisive.

In this chapter we shall examine student political values and ideologies from four perspectives: (1) how the majority of students view the state of the nation at the present time; (2) how the mainstream views have changed over the past few years; (3) how conservative and radical minority viewpoints express themselves in relation to the mainstream, and (4) how students' political values carry over to

49

identification with the Democratic and Republican Parties, and intentions to register and vote in the 1972 Presidential election.

Mainstream Views

The picture of American political life, as held by the student majority, may be sketched as follows: Students are pessimistic, discouraged, skeptical, and even cynical about the present political health of the nation and about the prospects for near-term improvement. They single out Vietnam, pollution, poverty, and racial prejudice as the main indicators that things are not working well in the country. They feel that our system of justice does not function evenhandedly, assuring petty criminals, tax exaders, polluters, war criminals and landlords of a fair trial and due process under the law, but not Black Panthers, dissenting servicemen, and antiwar leaders. They see certain groups singled out for discrimination and oppression, notably blacks, American Indians, Mexican-Americans, poor people, and longhaired students. They do not believe that our system of American democracy functions in practice as it is supposed to in theory. Rather, they believe that government is manipulated by special interests and that the mass of the public has been brainwashed into believing that what it thinks really counts. They hold that big business really runs the country, not the President, Congress, or the public; and they see business being derelict in its use of its awesome power, putting its selfish pursuit of profits ahead of the public well-being. They believe that some of our major institutions stand in need of drastic reform, including but not confined to the major political parties, the military, the penal system, and business.

Does this severe criticism of the country and the flaws in its political institutions add up to a radical ideology? Not at all. The underlying political values of students are moderate and traditional. The majority regards private property as inviolable, believes business *should* make a profit, and believes that social change should come about through working within the system in general and with the political-community-business Establishment in particular. The mainstream conviction holds that the system, while it may be flawed, is flexible and capable of whatever changes may be required.

In bringing about desirable change, outright violence—assaulting police, bombing buildings, destroying draft board records—is condemned. Tactics which might lead to violence but are not in themselves inherently violent are regarded with greater sympathy. Though the majority see the need for making major reforms in the society, only one out of three students places the desire to change society high on his own personal hierarchy of values. The wish to see someone else take on the burden of social change is far more universal than personal commitment to bringing it about.

Here, briefly and concretely, are some of the statistics that document and amplify the picture sketched in above:

State of the Nation

On the present state of the nation, student views are clearly pessimistic and skeptical:

—Six out of ten students (62%) think that things are going badly in the country.

—Only one out of ten believes that the war in Vietnam will be over by the 1972 Presidential election (13%), and an even smaller number (7%) thinks that even were the war in Vietnam to end today we could look forward to a period of peace. The vast majority subscribe to the belief that military involvements similar to Vietnam are "inevitable as a result of our present policies."

—A majority of those with an opinion on the matter think we are a sick society, while in 1968 the majority felt that the body politic was in sound health.

Signs That Things Are Not Working

In the pre-survey research, students named almost 40 reasons why they felt the body politic was in bad shape. In the survey each student was asked to select from among these the "really serious indications that things are not working as far as you are concerned."

The leading indicators of social malfunction, as students see them, are as follows:

51

—The Vietnam war (76%), pollution (71%), racial prejudice (62%), poverty (60%), drug addiction (54%), and crime (53%) are cited by the majority.

—More than four out of ten name waste and spending (47%), depletion of natural resources (45%), and lack of social justice (43%), as the prime indications of societal malfunction.

—Fewer than three out of ten students cite: the erosion of civil liberties (29%), the excessive influence of the mass media (24%), dependence on government handout (24%), the profit motive (23%), the decline of sexual morality (16%), the emphasis of technology (14%), decline in public services (12%), pornography (11%), and culture shock (9%).

Social Justice

Few topics arouse feelings as intense among students as the question of social justice. In the 1971 study, students were asked what groups in the society, if any, they felt were most oppressed and discriminated against.

Students' answers fall into a clear-cut pattern. The vast majority single out homosexuals (84%), blacks (81%), "longhairs" (76%), the poor (74%), American Indians (71%), and Mexican-Americans (68%) as the groups that are most oppressed and discriminated against. At the other extreme, few students believe that either "hard hats" (13%) or white Southerners (17%) are oppressed by our society. Interestingly, college students and women fall at the low end of the oppressed spectrum: only one out of four students thinks college students themselves are an oppressed group, and one out of three sees women as the subject of discrimination—and this despite high interest in the Women's Liberation Movement.

Institutional Change

In 1969, 1970, and 1971 the cross-section of students was asked which of our institutions most needed change. The institutions students evaluated were: the Congress, the political parties, the military, big business, the mass media, the universities, the trade unions, the foundations, the FBI, the penal system, the Constitution, and the

Supreme Court. For each institution four degrees of change were measured: no substantial change, moderate change, fundamental reform, and doing away with the institution altogether.

As of 1971, those institutions seen as needing no change or only moderate reform are: the Constitution (82%), the foundations (78%), the Supreme Court (76%), the mass media (67%), and the Congress (66%). At the other extreme are those institutions which large numbers of students believe should either be reformed in fundamental ways or done away with altogether. These are: the military (68%), the penal system (62%), the political parties (54%), and big business (46%). The universities, the trade unions, and the FBI lie between these two extremes.

Where the Power Is

For the first time this year students were asked the following question: "In your opinion where do you feel the real power in this country is vested?" Only one out of ten students states the "real power" lies with the general public. An equal number cites the CIA as the source of real power in the country. Twenty-three per cent name the President, 31% cite the Congress. The majority (58%) name the giant corporations and the financial institutions as the main sources of power in the country.

Consistent with this viewpoint, only a minority of students (42%) agreed with the following statement: "Our present system of government is largely democratic. Sooner or later the views of the people make themselves felt in important matters."

The majority (57%) reject the above statement in favor of this one: "Our present system of government is democratic in name only. The special interests run things and the mass of people are propagandized into believing that what they think really counts."

These answers suggest that the majority of students believe big business runs the country, manipulates the government, and brainwashes the public. In addition, the most widely held student criticism of American society is that business puts its pursuit of profits ahead of the public interest. Yet, alongside these Marxian perspectives there coexists another set of beliefs, equally widespread, that undercuts the classical socialist ideology: 85 per cent of all students believe that "business is entitled to make profit"—one of the most universally held beliefs uncovered by the study. Seven out of ten students believe that private property is sacrosanct and that destroying private property is morally reprehensible. Among the various signs that things are not working properly in the country, the profit motive ranks 23rd in a list of 36 indicators of societal malfunctions—far below most other issues.

Methods for Achieving Change

Consistent with the mainstream student stance of scathing criticism coupled with moderate prescriptions for bringing about change, the preferred methods for achieving meaningful social change are: the individual doing what he can in the community (78%) and working within the system (65%). Other methods endorsed by a majority of students include: seeking to change the values and outlook of the public, changing the values of those in power, stimulating the pressures of public opinion, and organizing minorities now excluded from power.

The more specifically political approaches such as changing the method of selecting candidates and organizing a new political party are endorsed by no more than ¼ to ⅓ of all students.

Near the bottom of the list are the most radical methods: creating conditions for revolution (11%), forcing those in power to adopt repressive measures in order to expose them (9%), and adopting tactics of harassment and confrontation (6%).

At the very bottom of the list, only 2 per cent go along with the idea that we should let things stay as they are.

Students' attitudes toward specific tactics are as follows:

—A majority (56%) say that they are unqualifiedly opposed to violence; a third would justify violence when all else fails (35%), and one out of ten students (9%), endorses violence as a general tactic.
—Tactics rejected unqualifiedly by the majority of the student body are: bombing or setting fire to buildings owned by large corporations (83%), destruction and mutilation of property (79%), holding authorities captive (74%), assaulting police (73%), and destroying draft board records (69%).
—On the other hand, a majority would occasionally justify sit-ins

54

(68%), giving ultimatums to those in authority (70%), shielding political prisoners (58%), resisting or disobeying the police (63%), and blockading buildings (55%).

Personal Commitment

Students were asked whether they would be willing to make a personal commitment such as devoting a year or two of their lives to doing something about the social problems that most concern them. One out of three students (34%) said they would be willing to make this kind of personal commitment to reduce pollution; 30% said they would do so to fight poverty; 25% cited bringing peace to Vietnam as a cause to which they could commit themselves; 23% would make a commitment to combating racism, and 22% favored controlling population as their commitment of choice. At much lower levels of commitments were the desire to reform our political institutions or change the social system (14%); to help legalize marijuana (9%), and fight for consumer's rights (8%).

The issues which win least personal commitment are: women's rights (4%) and revenue sharing (2%).

Students were asked in 1970 and again in 1971 whether in making a personal commitment of time and effort they would prefer to work with the protest movement or the Establishment. The answers to this question in both years are virtually identical. Two out of ten students prefer to work with the protest movement (18% in 1970 and 19% in 1971), and five out of ten choose the Establishment (49% in 1970 and 53% in 1971). (The balance of students rejected both alternatives or said it made no difference to them one way or the other.)

Local community leaders were, by a wide margin, the No. 1 choice of partners within the Establishment. All other categories of Establishment leaders, including business leaders, members of Congress, members of the federal and state government, and candidates for political office, took second place to local community leaders.

Interestingly, there have been some changes since last year, mainly toward a somewhat greater preference for working with members of the government—in Congress and at the state and federal levels of the executive branch.

Recent Changes

A dimension of depth can be added to this picture of current student political views by seeing it in a time perspective. Several patterns of change emerge when we inspect the findings of 1971 against those of the past few years. The 1971 findings have shown that students hold a generally gloomy and pessimistic political outlook. Yet, when we inspect their specific and detailed criticisms of the society and the tactics they would endorse for bringing about social and political change, we find that with few exceptions, their criticisms are less extreme and less radical than in the previous year. One pattern repeats itself over and over again. From 1969 to 1970, student anger and radicalism increases sharply; from 1970 to 1971, the anger and radicalism falls off, dropping almost but not quite to the 1969 level.

This pattern holds true of these student criticisms:

—Big business is too preoccupied with its own profits for the public interest;
—Economic well-being is "unjustly and unfairly distributed";
—Our foreign policy reflects our narrow and selfish interests;
—We are a racist nation;
—Vietnam is an expression of "pure imperialism";
—Our democratic system is not adequately responsive to the needs of our people;
—Many of our major institutions—the universities, the military, big business, the trade unions—stand in need of fundamental reform.

In each instance, the level of student criticism grew sharply in 1970 and fell back in 1971. The fallback, however, was not complete, in most instances settling part way between the 1969 and 1970 levels.

The pullback from extremist criticism is even more marked in those few instances where the radicalism level falls below that of 1969. Thus, we find less feeling now than in previous years that the Establishment unfairly controls our lives; that the individual in our society is isolated and cut off from others; that the two-party system offers no valid alternative; that blacks, radicals, and protesters cannot receive a fair trial; and that the tactics of overt violence such as de-

56

stroying draft board records and setting fire to buildings owned by corporations can be justified. Several years ago most students vehemently rejected the use of force by police to curb disorders; today, the resistance to police force has diminished markedly.

In a few instances, student sentiment has moved toward greater radicalism, or at least toward greater skepticism. There is more negative criticism of the FBI than in the past. And there is less opposition to creating a revolutionary party or to the idea that Vietnam is an imperialistic adventure. As ideological passions cool, students seem less ready to reject any ideas from either end of the political spectrum.

Minority Viewpoints

In the preceding sections of this chapter we examined mainstream student views and changes over the past several years. Let us now briefly describe minority viewpoints at the two extremes of the political spectrum.

The majority sets the tempo and tone of the present political climate on campus: sharpness in criticism, moderation in prescription for change. But at both ends of the political spectrum, we find clear-cut patterns of political belief that are less moderate and more passionately ideological in tone.

On the conservative end of the spectrum, more than one out of ten students (generally between 10% and 20%) holds the following beliefs:

—The country is too concerned with equality at the expense of law and order and too concerned with the "welfare bum," at the expense of the hard-working person struggling to make a living.
—The police should not hesitate to use force to curb disorders.
—If there is malfunctioning in the society, it is due to an overemphasis on pornography and sexual license, the decline of religion and morals, and the excessive dependence on government handouts.
—Our foreign policy is *not* too narrow and selfish; economic well-being is *not* unjustly and unfairly distributed; we are *not* racists; and the war in Vietnam is *not* imperialistic.
—The Supreme Court and the foundations stand in need of funda-

mental reform; the FBI, Congress, the universities, and big business require no change.

—Shielding prisoners, giving ultimatums to authorities, and resisting or disobeying the police can never be justified as tactics to achieve change, whatever the cause.

—We should assure the viability of a non-Communist government in Vietnam before ending the war; no one should be held responsible for incidents such as My Lai since they are inevitable in warfare.

—Meaningful social change in the country can best be created by cracking down on draft-resisters, encouraging more respect for the flag, and increasing respect for the police and other authorities.

The emphasis on law and order, respect for the police and sentiment for cracking down on "welfare cheats" is, it should be noted, not confined to a small conservative minority. It is held at the 40% level or higher.

Radical Beliefs

On the radical end of the political spectrum, one out of ten or more students holds the following beliefs:

—The individual is isolated and cut off by our society; the Establishment controls our lives and we can never be free until we are rid of it; freedom cannot be achieved by the individual within the present framework of today's society.

—Social change can best be achieved by working outside the system within the protest movement, creating a greater class consciousness, a mass revolutionary party, and the other conditions necessary for revolution.

—Violent methods are sometimes necessary, if the cause is justified, including destroying draft board records, holding authorities captive, bombing buildings, setting fire to buildings owned by large corporations, stealing, selling dope, destroying private—or public—property, and assaulting or resisting the police. No one should be punished for violating a law he doesn't agree with.

—The political parties, the military, and the FBI should be done away with altogether.

58

Party Affiliation and Intention to Vote

Let us conclude this chapter by turning now from ideology to practical politics. How many students are conservative, moderate, liberal, or radical? How many consider themselves as belonging to a major political party? How many are Democrats or Republicans? How many intend to register and to vote in the 1972 election? Fortunately, the answers to these questions are clear-cut and highly informative in the light of the preceding discussion.

Self-Classifications

Students were asked to classify themselves as conservative, moderate, liberal or radical, regardless of party affiliation. Twenty-one per cent categorized themselves as conservative, 44% as middle-of-the-road, 25% as liberal, and 10% as radical. Two out of three conservatives qualified their conservatism as being of the moderate variety. The majority of the middle-of-the-roaders qualified their position as middle-of-the-road leaning toward liberal.

Significantly, in answering an identical question posed in 1970, the students gave just about the same responses (see Table 44). These findings serve to qualify the students' self-image of their own mood as having turned away from conservatism toward radicalism.

Since the beginning of the Yankelovich studies of student values, essentially the same political pattern has prevailed. At the two extremes, conservatives outnumber radicals two to one. Radicals comprise about one out of ten students and conservatives about two out of ten. The vast majority in the middle divides between moderate and liberal and swings in one direction or another depending on circumstances. The dominant campus position today is middle-of-the-road, listing slightly to the Left.

When we turn to the question of affiliation with the two major political parties, several important findings emerge:

—Over the past several years there has been a large-scale shift away from party allegiance. In 1969, about 1 out of 5 students (23%) said that they belonged to no major political party. In 1970 and

1971, almost two out of five (37%) rejected any party affiliation.

—Most of the erosion has come at the expense of the Democratic Party. In 1969, 47% of the students said they were Democrats and 25% said they were Republicans. In 1971, 36% say they are Democrats and 21% say they are Republicans. The Democrats have lost a full quarter of their student allies. These students have not, however, joined the Republican Party. They have dropped all political party affiliations.

—The erosion of party loyalty does not, however, mean that students will fail to exercise their political franchise. On the contrary, a full 90% of all students say that they are either now registered to vote or intend to register in the future. Moreover, virtually everyone who intends to register also intends to vote in the 1972 election. Whether or not they will vote depends on many circumstances, but as a reflection of attitudes and values it is significant that 88% of all students expect to vote in the 1972 Presidential race. The campus could well have a decisive influence on the outcome of the election.

Tables 21 to 45 which follow present these various findings in greater detail.

Table **21.** How Things Are Going in the Nation*

	Total Students 1971**	
	%	
Things in the country are going		
Very well	1	
Fairly well	34	
Pretty badly	47	62
Very badly	15	
Not sure	3	

* **Question 1a:** "Generally, how do you feel that things are going in the country today—very well, fairly well, pretty badly, or very badly?"

** Asked only in 1971.

Table 22.   If the Vietnam War Were to End Today . . .*
(Also see page 230)

	Total Students 1971**
	%
We could look forward to a period of peace	►7
Similar military involvements are inevitable as a result of present policies	68
Not sure/depends	25

* **Question 4b:** "If the Vietnam war were to end today, do you feel that we could look forward to a period of peace or do you feel similar future involvements are almost inevitable as a result of our present policies?"
** Asked only in 1971.

Table 23.   Whether the War Will End Soon and the Economy Will Pick Up*

	Total Students 1971**
	%
The war in Vietnam will be over by the next Presidential election ..	13
Economic conditions in the country will improve this year	26

* **Question 1b:** "Do you think that:"
** Asked only in 1971.

Table 24.   Are We a "Sick Society"?*
(Also see page 231)

	Total Students	
	1971**	1968
	%	%
Agree that we are a "sick society"	45	40
Disagree that we are a "sick society"	►38	►54
Not sure	17	6

* **Question 5a:** "Some people are calling this country a 'sick society.' Do you agree or disagree with them?"
** Asked only in 1971 and 1968.

Table 25. Extent of Agreement with Criticisms Made About American Society*
(Also see page 232)

	Total Students		
	1971	1970	1969**
	%	%	%
Business is too concerned with profits and not public responsibility			
Strongly agree	►55	►61	►50
Partially agree	38	34	44
Disagree	7	5	6
Our foreign policy is based on our own narrow economic and power interests			
Strongly agree	►35	►48	►31
Partially agree	53	40	53
Disagree	12	12	16
Economic well-being in this country is unjustly and unfairly distributed			
Strongly agree	►34	►41	►33
Partially agree	48	48	50
Disagree	18	11	17
Basically, we are a racist nation			
Strongly agree	►37	►53	►38
Partially agree	44	36	40
Disagree	19	11	22
Today's American society is characterized by "injustice, insensibility, lack of candor, and inhumanity"			
Strongly agree	►21	►26	►15
Partially agree	48	48	50
Disagree	31	26	35
The war in Vietnam is pure imperialism			
Strongly agree	►24	►41	►16
Partially agree	48	38	40
Disagree	28	21	44

(Continued on next page)

* **Question 6:** "This card lists a number of criticisms that have been made in recent years about American society. For each one, will you tell me whether you strongly agree, partially agree, or whether you strongly disagree?"
** Question not asked in 1968.

POLITICAL VALUES AND IDEOLOGIES

	Total Students		
	1971	1970	1969**
	%	%	%
Morally and spiritually our country has lost its way†			
Strongly agree	20	—	18
Partially agree	46	—	45
Disagree	34	—	37
The individual in today's society is isolated and cut off from meaningful relationships with others			
Strongly agree	19	14	15
Partially agree	45	38	44
Disagree	►36	►48	►41
Computer and other advances in technology are creating an inhuman and impersonal world			
Strongly agree	21	20	18
Partially agree	46	47	46
Disagree	33	33	36
The American system of representative democracy can respond effectively to the needs of the people			
Strongly agree	27	24	27
Partially agree	59	54	60
Disagree	►14	►22	►13
The Establishment unfairly controls every aspect of our lives. We can never be free until we are rid of it			
Strongly agree	11	8	8
Partially agree	35	50	50
Disagree	►54	►42	►42
The two-party system offers no real alternative‡			
Strongly agree	►29	►38	—
Partially agree	44	46	—
Disagree	27	16	—

(Continued on next page)

---

† Question not asked in 1970.
‡ Question not asked in 1969.

	Total Students		
	1971	1970	1969**
	%	%	%
There is more concern today for the "welfare bum" who doesn't want to work, than for the hard-working person who is struggling to make a living†			
Strongly agree	34	—	31
Partially agree	34	—	38
Disagree	32	—	31
There is too much concern with equality and too little with law and order†			
Strongly agree	17	—	17
Partially agree	32	—	40
Disagree	►51	—	►43
Minority must not be allowed to impose will on majority†			
Strongly agree	18	—	18
Partially agree	34	—	45
Disagree	►48	—	►37
Police should not hesitate to use force to maintain order†			
Strongly agree	16	—	5
Partially agree	38	—	27
Disagree	►46	—	►68
People's privacy is being destroyed°			
Strongly agree	36	—	—
Partially agree	47	—	—
Disagree	17	—	—
A mass revolutionary party should be created†			
Strongly agree	11	—	5
Partially agree	22	—	14
Disagree	►67	—	►81
Radicals of Left as much a threat to rights of individuals as radicals of Right†			
Strongly agree	48	—	54
Partially agree	39	—	36
Disagree	13	—	10

(Continued on next page)

° Question asked only in 1971.

	Total Students		
	1971	1970	1969**
	%	%	%
You can never achieve freedom within the frame-work of contemporary American society°			
Strongly agree	15	—	—
Partially agree	39	—	—
Disagree	46	—	—
No one should be punished for violating a law he feels is immoral°			
Strongly agree	13	—	—
Partially agree	42	—	—
Disagree	45	—	—

Table **26.**   The Most Significant Signs That Things
Are Not Working Properly*
(Also see page 233)

	Total Students 1971**
	%
Significant signs that things are not working properly today	
The Vietnam War	►76
Pollution	►71
Racial prejudice	►62
Poverty	►60
Drug addiction	►54
Rising crime	►53
Lack of concern	48
Amount of waste and spending	47

(Continued on next page)

---

* **Question 5b:** "Here's a deck of cards that lists some of the factors people have men-tioned as significant indications that things are not working properly today. Will you go through the deck and put into one pile just the really serious indications that things are not working as far as you are concerned?"
** Asked only in 1971.

	Total Students 1971**
	%
Depletion of natural resources	45
Lack of social justice	43
Power of industrial-military complex	42
Emphasis on money	40
Deterioration of the cities	39
Corruption	37
Failure to keep pace	31
Concentration of wealth	30
Low voter turnout	29
Erosion of civil liberties	29
Lack of leadership	28
Respect for authority eroded	27
Crackdown on dissent	25
No long-range planning	25
Excessive influence of mass media	24
Dependence on government handouts	24
Profit motive	23
Wiretapping	23
Quality of life	23
Polarization	21
Decline in religion	21
Generation gap	19
Treatment of the aged	19
Commercialism	18
Decline in sexual morality	16
Emphasis on technology	14
Decline in civility	13
Declining public services	12
Emphasis on pornography	11
Cultural shock	9
All of these	2

Table **27.**   Where the Real Power in the Country Is Vested*
(Also see page 234)

	Total Students 1971**
	%
The real power in the country lies with:	
The giant corporation	►51
Congress	31
Financiers and financial institutions	►26
The President	23
The Defense Department	21
The interplay of diverse special interest groups, such as labor, religious leaders, and educators	15
The general public	10
The CIA	10
The Democratic party	3
The technocrats	5
The Republican party	3
Other	2
Not sure	7

* **Question 4c:** "In your opinion, where do you feel the real power in this country is vested?"
** Asked only in 1971.

Table **28.**   Whether or Not We have a Real Democracy*
(Also see page 235)

	Total Students 1971**
	%
Our present system of government is largely democratic. Sooner or later the views of the people make themselves felt in important matters	42
Our present system of government is democratic in name only. The special interests run things and the mass of people are propagandized that what they think really counts	►58

* **Question 21:** "If you had to make a choice, which one of these two statements best describes your views?"
** Asked only in 1971.

Table 29.   Attitudes Toward American Society and Way of Life*

(Also see page 236)

	Total Students		
	1971	1970	1969**
	%	%	%
The American way of life is superior to that of any other country	12	10	17
There are serious flaws in our society today, but the system is flexible enough to solve them ...	61	68	70
The American system is not flexible enough; radical change is needed	19	22	13
The whole social system ought to be replaced by an entirely new one. The existing structures are too rotten for repair†	8	—	—

* **Question 9a:** "Which one of the following views of American society and American life best reflects your own feelings?"
** Question not asked in 1968.
† Asked only in 1971.

Table **30.**   What Groups Are Oppressed and Discriminated
Against?*

	Total Students 1971**
	%
Groups that are oppressed	
Homosexuals	►84
The blacks	►81
Longhairs	►76
The poor	►74
American Indians	►71
Mexican-Americans	►68
High school dropouts	54
Women	33
College students	27
White Southerners	17
Hard hats	13

* **Question 7b:** "Generally, do you think of [READ LIST] as being members of an oppressed
or discriminated group in our society or not?"
** Asked only in 1971.

Table 31. How Well Justice Functions: What Groups Are Not Assured of a Fair Trial?*

	Total Students	
	1971	1970**
	%	%
Definitely believe the following cannot be assured a fair trial		
Black Panthers	65	71
Moratorium leaders	53	43
Dissenting servicemen†	51	—
Homosexuals†	51	—
Radicals	►49	►60
Weathermen	49	47
College protesters	►46	►54
Drug addicts	46	50
Conscientious objectors	45	52
Drug pushers	45	40
Student activists†	42	—
Indians	40	41
Mexican-Americans†	37	—
Mafia members	33	41
Members of the Klan†	31	—
Prostitutes	30	—
Middle-class blacks	►29	►41
Strike leaders	26	30
Polluters†	25	—
Tax evaders	20	22
Petty criminals	19	28
Manufacturers of defective products	18	14
War criminals†	16	—
Landlords	13	11

* **Question 7a:** "How well do you feel that social justice functions in this country? For instance, do you think that [READ LIST] can be assured of a fair trial and judicial process?"
** Asked only in 1971 and 1970.
† Not asked in 1970.

Table **32.**   Institutions That Most Need Change*
(Also see pages 237–238)

	Total Students		
	1971	1970	1969**
	%	%	%
The Constitution†			
No substantial change	49	47	—
Moderate change	33	37	—
Fundamental reform	15	14	—
Done away with	3	2	—
The Supreme Court†			
No substantial change	33	27	—
Moderate change	43	40	—
Fundamental reform	▶21	▶30	—
Done away with	3	3	—
Foundations‡			
No substantial change	30	—	—
Moderate change	48	—	—
Fundamental reform	18	—	—
Done away with	4	—	—
The FBI†			
No substantial change	26	40	—
Moderate change	35	29	—
Fundamental reform	▶29	▶19	—
Done away with	10	12	—
The mass media			
No substantial change	19	19	18
Moderate change	48	45	46
Fundamental reform	30	34	33
Done away with	3	2	3
Congress†			
No substantial change	18	17	—
Moderate change	48	45	—
Fundamental reform	32	35	—
Done away with	2	3	—

(Continued on next page)

* **Question 8:** "Which one of the descriptions on this card do you feel best describes each of the following institutions?"
** Question not asked in 1968.   ‡ Question asked only in 1971.
† Question not asked in 1969.

71

	Total Students		
	1971	**1970**	**1969****
	%	%	%
The universities			
No substantial change	14	5	11
Moderate change	50	52	57
Fundamental reform	►35	►42	►32
Done away with	1	1	—
Trade unions			
No substantial change	11	7	14
Moderate change	50	45	43
Fundamental reform	►32	►40	►32
Done away with	7	8	11
Big business			
No substantial change	10	8	10
Moderate change	44	42	52
Fundamental reform	►40	►45	►35
Done away with	6	5	3
The political parties			
No substantial change	8	7	9
Moderate change	38	26	33
Fundamental reform	44⎱ 54	50⎱ 67	49⎱ 58
Done away with	10⎰	17⎰	9⎰
The penal system†			
No substantial change	8	5	—
Moderate change	30	26	—
Fundamental reform	57	62	—
Done away with	5	7	—
The military			
No substantial change	5	5	10
Moderate change	27	23	29
Fundamental reform	57	56	50
Done away with	11	16	11

Table 33.   Social Problems of Greatest Personal Concern*

	Total Students 1971 %
Bringing peace to Vietnam	►56
Reducing pollution	►40
Fighting poverty	29
Controlling population	27
Combating racism	23
Curbing inflation	20
Reducing hard drug addiction	16
Reforming the judicial system	15
Combating crime	15
Aid to higher education	15
Reforming our political institutions	15
Changing the social system	15
Legalizing abortions	15
Welfare reform	14
Defending consumers' rights	10
Bringing peace to the Middle East	9
Limiting the arms race	9
Legalizing marijuana	9
Winning women's rights	5
Helping the third world	4
Revenue sharing	2

* **Question 2a:** "Which two or three problems or issues facing the country concern you personally the most?"

Table **34.**   Social Problems to Whose Solution the Student
Is Willing to Commit a Year or Two of His Life*
(Also see page 239)

	Total Students 1971 %
Reducing pollution	►34
Fighting poverty	►30
Bringing peace to Vietnam	►25
Combating racism	►23
Controlling population	►22
Reducing hard drug addiction	19
Reforming the political institutions	14
Changing the social system	14
Combating crime	13
Legalizing abortions	13
Aid to higher education	12
Reforming the judicial system	11
Welfare reform	11
Legalizing marijuana	9
Consumers' rights	8
Curbing inflation	8
Bringing peace to the Middle East	7
Limiting the arms race	6
Helping the third world	6
Winning women's rights	4
Revenue sharing	2

* **Question 2b:** "Would you be willing to make a personal commitment such as devoting a
year or two of your life to doing something about any of these issues?"

Table **35.**   Best Methods for Achieving Meaningful Social Change*

(Also see page 240)

	Total Students 1971**
	%
Individual doing what he can in community	►78
Working within the system	►65
Pressures of public opinion	56
Changing values and outlook of public	55
Organize minorities now excluded	55
Change values of those in power	52
Crack down on welfare cheats	45
Create respect for law and order	41
Give local community power and control	40
Respect for police and other authority	39
New government legislation rigorously enforced	36
Changing method of selecting political candidates	34
Decentralized power, federal to local government	26
Organize new political party	25
Nationalize natural resources	24
Having more respect for flag	24
Nationalize private industry	15
Create class consciousness	14
Cracking down on draft resisters	11
Create conditions for revolution	11
Force those in power to adopt repressive measures to expose them	9
Adopt tactics of harassment and confrontation	6
Let things continue as they are	2

* **Question 19:** "Which of these comes closest to your own point of view? The best methods for achieving meaningful social change in the country are:"
** Asked only in 1971.

Table 36. Is It Best to Work Outside or Inside the System?*
(Also see page 241)

	Total Students 1971**
	%
Best to work:	
Outside the system	10
Within the system	►75
Not sure	15

* **Question 13f:** "Do you feel an individual who believes in changing society can do more by living 'outside' the traditional social structure or by working from 'within'?"
** Asked only in 1971.

Table 37. Personal Preference for Working with the Establishment or the Protest Movement*
(Also see page 242)

	Total Students	
	1971**	1970
	%	%
Prefer to work with:		
Protest movement	19	18
Establishment	53	49
No difference	13	14
Neither	14	18
Don't know	1	1

* **Question 2c:** "If you were to commit yourself to this type of activity, would you sooner work as part of a protest movement or part of the Establishment?"
** Asked only in 1971 and 1970.

Table **38.**   Preferred "Partner" Within the Establishment*

	Total Students	
	1971**	1970
	%	%
Prefer to work with:		
Community leaders	41	39
Business leaders	18	15
Members of Congress	►15	►10
Federal agencies and departments	15	13
Federal government	►14	►6
Candidates for political office	12	8
State government	►11	►4
Members of the executive branch of the federal government	9	5
Other (voluntary, youth, all other organizations)	6	15
None	8	—

* **Question 2d:** "If you had to choose, whom would you most prefer to work with jointly on this type of activity?"
** Asked only in 1971.

Table **39.**   Use of Violence*

	Total Students 1971**
	%
Violent means are often necessary	9 ⎫
Violence is justified, but only when all else fails	35 ⎬ 44
I am opposed to violence	56 ⎭

* Question 18: "Which of these statements best expresses your feelings about the use of violence?"
** Asked only in 1971.

Table **40.**   Justifiable Tactics*

	Total Students		
	1971	1970	1969**
	%	%	%
Sit-ins			
Always justified	►26	►22	►12
Sometimes justified	68	69	78
Never justified	6	9	10
Shielding political prisoners†			
Always justified	13	—	—
Sometimes justified	58	—	—
Never justified	29	—	—
Ultimatums to those in authority			
Always justified	10	9	6
Sometimes justified	70	76	75
Never justified	►20	►15	►19
Destroying draft board records‡			
Always justified	9	6	—
Sometimes justified	22	17	—
Never justified	►69	►77	—
Blockades of buildings			
Always justified	5	3	2
Sometimes justified	55	54	46
Never justified	►40	►43	►52
Resisting or disobeying police			
Always justified	4	3	1
Sometimes justified	63	62	62
Never justified	33	35	37
Assaulting police			
Always justified	4	1	—
Sometimes justified	23	26	21
Never justified	73	73	79

(Continued on next page)

* **Question 17b:** "Which of the tactics on the card do you feel are always justifiable, which are sometimes justifiable and which do you feel are never justifiable?"
** Not asked in 1968.
† Asked only in 1971.   ‡ Not asked in 1969.

	Total Students		
	1971	1970	1969**
	%	%	%
Bombing or setting fire to buildings owned by large corporations‡			
Always justified	4	1	—
Sometimes justified	13	11	—
Never justified	83	88	—
Destruction or mutilation of property			
Always justified	3	1	—
Sometimes justified	18	18	16
Never justified	79	81	84
Holding an authority captive			
Always justified	3	1	1
Sometimes justified	23	28	21
Never justified	74	71	78

Table **41.**   Tactics in Regard to Vietnam*

	Total Students 1971**
	%
We must first insure a non-Communist government in South Vietnam	10
We must first have an orderly transfer of responsibility from United States troops to the South Vietnamese	40
We should leave now	45
None	2
Other	3

* **Question 3a:** "Most people agree that we should get out of Vietnam—but there are different views about how and when we should leave. Which one view most closely resembles your own viewpoint?"
** Asked only in 1971.

Table **42.**   Moral Position in Relation to My Lai*

	Total Students 1971**
	%
We are all responsible	►40
This kind of thing is inevitable and no one is responsible	►27
The commanding officer	27
The individual soldier or officer such as Lieutenant Calley	25
The United States general in charge of the campaign	18
The President of the United States	18
The Secretary of Defense	13
Don't know	1

* **Question 4a:** "What is your own moral position as far as the Vietnam war is concerned? For example, in instances such as the My Lai affair, who do you think must be held responsible?"
** Asked only in 1971.

Table **43.**   Voter Registration and Intentions to Vote*
(Also see page 243)

	Total Students 1971
	%
Registration	
Now registered to vote	37 ⎫ 90
Intend to register	53 ⎬
Do not intend to register	10 ⎭
Intention to vote	
Expect to vote in 1972 elections	►**88**
Do not expect to vote in 1972	12

* **Questions O, P, Q:** "Are you registered to vote? [IF NOT] Do you plan to register for the 1972 elections? [IF REGISTERED OR PLAN TO REGISTER] Do you expect to cast your vote in the 1972 elections?"

Table **44.**   Self-Identification as Conservative, Moderate, Liberal, or Radical*
(Also see page 244)

	Total Students	
	1971	1970
	%	%
Conservative	7	5
Moderate/conservative	14	17
Moderate/middle of the road	16	18
Liberal/middle of the road	28	29
Liberal	25	23
Radical	10	8

* **Question R:** "Regardless of any party affiliation, do you think of yourself as:"

81

Table 45. Self-Identification with Political Parties*
(Also see page 245)

	Total Students		
	1971	1970	1969**
	%	%	%
Democratic	►36	►35	►47
Republican	21	22	25
Other	6	6	5
None	37	37	23

* **Question N:** "Which political party do you identify with most closely?"
** Not asked in 1968.

CHAPTER 6

Alienation

IN THE PRECEDING two chapters we described the changing cultural and political values of the college student population. We found each of these two worlds of values forming a different pattern: the world of cultural values now moves toward ever more advanced forms of expression and experimentation in matters of sex, marriage, religion, relation to work, money, authority, nature, and career; the world of political values moves in the opposite direction, away from activism, violence, and involvement.

But the two worlds are, of course, facets of a single unity since they express various aspects of student life experience. Let us now inspect those findings of the research which show what effect these changing values have on the students' feelings of belonging to or alienation from a society that is not advancing at the same tempo, and in many instances is not even moving in the same direction as they are. Are college students alienated from the larger society, as many observers have claimed? Have their changing personal, social and political values driven them out of the mainstream of American society?

We have had a partial answer in the last chapter. The almost universal student intention to vote in the 1972 election is hardly an expression of alienation or dropping out of the society. And yet this answer by itself is misleading. For there are indications, spread throughout the research, that a substantial number of students are alienated, some of them deeply so.

Drawing from student responses to a wide variety of questions, we estimate that about 30 per cent of the student body is alienated to some degree, and that from a third to a half of this group is deeply alienated. Furthermore, these numbers underestimate the total since they do not include students who have already dropped out of college.

83

Here are the questions and responses to them on which our estimates are based:

Would-Be Exiles

Students were asked, "Is there any other country or society you think you might prefer to live in?" In answer to this question, three out of ten students (30%) said that they would prefer to live in some other country. (The countries named are Australia, the countries of Western Europe, Scandinavia, and Canada. There are also a small number of students who mention Cuba and the Soviet Union.)

Shared Values

Each year since 1969 students were asked whether they felt that their own personal values and points of view were shared by most other Americans. This year, 32 per cent of the students answered with an unqualified "no," down from 40 per cent in 1970 and 36 per cent in 1969. On the other hand, the number of those who just aren't sure whether or not their values are shared by their fellow Americans has increased over the past three years. This finding is yet another illustration of a pattern we have seen throughout these discussions—a moving away from sharp polarization, with its ideologically rooted certainties, toward uncertainty and confusion.

Acceptance of the "American Way of Life"

In a related question, students were asked to select which one of four statements best reflected their own personal feelings. The four statements and responses to them are:

—"The American way of life is superior to that of any other country." Twelve per cent of the students chose this statement.
—"There are serious flaws in our society today but the system is flexible enough to solve them." Sixty-one per cent selected this statement.

—"The American system is not flexible enough. Radical change is needed." Nineteen per cent selected this statement.

—"The whole social system ought to be replaced by an entirely new one. The existing structures are too rotten for repair." Eight per cent chose this statement.

These figures give yet another dimension of student relationship to the society. One out of ten sees no flaws in the country; six out of ten see serious flaws but think we can handle them without basic structural change; and three out of ten would press for drastic change with varying degrees of radical revolutionary conviction.

Turning from the political to the personal, we find a strikingly similar distribution of student sentiment to the choice of life styles offered by the society. Two out of ten (17%) say they would like "just about the same kind of life for myself as my parents have." Five out of ten (49%) anticipate no great difficulty in "accepting the kind of life the society has to offer—a good job, marriage, children, living in a pleasant community and becoming part of the community." The other three out of ten are divided between those who accept the conventional way of life with difficulty and reluctance but don't see any alternative (18%), and those who find "the prospect of accepting a conventional way of life in the society as it now exists intolerable" (15%).

In brief, then, however we look at the data from either the personal, cultural, or political perspective, we find a seven-out-of-ten majority moving without acute discomfort into the mainstream of society. The other three out of ten feel a greater sense of strain and experience some degree of alienation. The alienation takes a variety of forms, including radical politics, radical changes in life style, dropping out of the mainstream into the counterculture and withdrawal into an intense form of privatism and disengagement.

With Tables 46 through 50 which now follow, we complete our broad-brush description of the values and beliefs of college students as a whole. In the next series of chapters we take a more analytical approach, examining the various demographic and non-demographic subgroups that make up this heterogeneous population of more than 8,000,000 men and women.

Table 46. Feeling That One's Personal Values Are Shared by Other Americans*

	Total Students		
	1971	1970	1969**
	%	%	%
Personal values shared by other Americans			
Yes	30	42	33
No	▶32	▶40	▶36
Not certain	38	18	31

* **Question 22a:** "In general, do you feel your personal values and point of view are shared by most Americans today?"
** Not asked in 1968.

Table 47. Feeling That One's Values and Point of View Are Represented by Our Government*

	Total Students 1971**
	%
Values represented by our government	
Yes	▶16
No	25
Not sure	59

* **Question 22c:** "Do you think that your values and point of view are represented by our government?"
* Asked only in 1971.

Table 48.   Other Countries and Societies the Individual
             Might Prefer to Live in*

	Total Students 1971**
	%
Would prefer to live in another society	30
Country would prefer to live in	
Australia	23
Western Europe	22
Scandinavia	19
Canada	18
Great Britain	9
Israel	5
Africa	5
USSR	3
Cuba	2

* Question 14b: "Is there any other country or society that you think you might prefer to live in?"
  Question 14c: "Which society or country do you think you might prefer to live in?"
** Asked only in 1971.

Table 49.   Groups with Which the Individual Identifies*

	Total Students 1971
	%
Identify with	
Students	82
Other people of your generation	64
Your family	61
The middle class	49
Liberals	30
People of your nationality	29
People of your religion	27

(Continued on next page)

* Question 23: "With which of the following groups, if any, do you feel a sense of identification?"

	Total Students 1971
	%
People of your race	27
People of your neighborhood	24
Working class	22
Conservatives	16
The movement	13
Counterculture	11
The New Left	11
The Old Left	3

Table **50.**   Acceptance of Life Styles Offered by the Society*
(Also see page 246)

	Total Students 1971**
	%
I would like just about the same kind of life for myself as my parents have	17
I anticipate no great difficulty in accepting the kind of life the society has to offer—a good job, marriage, children, living in a pleasant community, and becoming part of the community	49
It's not going to be easy for me to accept the conventional job-marriage-children-home of your own kind of life, but I don't see any other alternative	18
I find the prospect of accepting a conventional way of life in the society as it now exists intolerable	►15
Don't know	1

* Question 14a: "Which of these phrases best describes your own feelings?"
** Asked only in 1971. (Repercentaged to add to 100% as some respondents chose more than one answer.)

PART II
Profiles

CHAPTER 7

The Psychology of Affluence

THUS FAR we have treated the student body as a monolith—as if it were a homogeneous population of 8,000,000 students moving together as a single force, and possessed of a single mind. We have focused virtually all of our attention on the mainstream of student opinion. Now in this second section we turn to some of the ways students differ from each other. There is, as we shall see, much understanding to be gained from shifting our perspective and looking at the student body from the point of view of its heterogeneity.

In this series of chapters in Part II we present five profiles of student groups:

PROFILE 1. Students who attend college mainly for practical reasons, as a means for advancing their careers, their income, and their social status, compared with students who, taking affluence for granted, are less concerned with the practical benefits of their college education than with intangibles. (This profile is in the present chapter.)

PROFILE 2. Students who identify with the New Left compared with above-mentioned two groups. (Chapter 8.)

PROFILE 3. A comparison of students who identify with the Republican Party, the Democratic Party and no major political party. (Chapter 9.)

PROFILE 4.   The men compared with the women. (Chapter 10.)

PROFILE 5.   Blacks and other non-white students compared with the white students. (Chapter 11.)

These profiles are but a fraction of the many possible breakdowns of the college population. Out of the variety we have inspected, they appear to be the most significant.

The Career-Minded and the Post-Affluent

Each student has his own reasons for going to college. Some yield to family pressures, others attend college because not going never occurred to them, others struggle and sacrifice to fulfill a long-held dream of higher education. Some students are highly motivated; some just drift along. But the most widely held reason for going to college is to advance practical career goals—work, money, success, position in the society.

Before this present series of studies was launched, research in the mid-1960's showed that many students had begun to search for more intangible benefits from their college education, having to do with self-expression, self-fulfillment, self-actualization, and societal change. We found that students so motivated did not, for the most part, overtly reject the practical side of college. They, too, expected to have careers, a good income, and a comfortable niche in the social structure. But they played down these latter values. Their attitude was the opposite of the old Depression psychology of being haunted by the specter of economic insecurity. They were motivated instead by a *psychology of affluence* that placed economic security low on the hierarchy of values. Shunting aside what they regarded as our society's obsession with money, success, and security, they reached gropingly toward new goals, new styles of life.

Recognizing that this motivation, always present in the few, seemed now to dominate the thinking of the many, perhaps even a majority in some colleges, we sought a method for measuring their number and comparing their views with those of their more traditional peers. After a period of experimentation, the best method turned out to be the simplest. Our pre-survey research had provided us with the words and phrases students use when describing their own reasons for attending college. We crystallized these into two prototypical statements as follows:

STATEMENT #1:

"For me college is mainly a practical matter. With a college education I can earn more money, have a more interesting career, and enjoy a better position in the society."

STATEMENT #2:

"I'm not really concerned with the practical benefits of college. I suppose I take them for granted. College for me is something more intangible; perhaps the opportunity to change things rather than make out well within the existing system."

Each student in these surveys was asked to pick one of the two statements that came closest to his own motivations for attending college. Only a tiny handful had difficulty in doing so. The students in each group were then compared on a wide variety of values relating to politics, religion, sex, patriotism, work, family, and similar matters.

No other basis for differentiating students—neither sex, nor race, nor family background, nor field of major—discriminates quite as sharply as these different motivations for attending college. This has been confirmed in study after study.

In 1968 the practical Career-Minded group remained the majority, 56 per cent of all students falling into this category. But 44 per cent of the students, projecting to more than 3,000,000 men and women, fell into the more intangible, Affluence-for-Granted camp. The next year, in 1969, the proportions remained the same. In 1970 and 1971 a slight shift occurred, and we now have an even larger majority of the Career-Minded (61%). We attach no great significance to this shift, except to note that the number of those who take affluence for granted these days has certainly not increased.

The importance of distinguishing between the Career-Minded and those whose goals are more intangible is not merely that their attitudes and values on many matters differ. That might well be expected, given the fundamental character of the motivations that divide them. It is the nature of the differences that capture our attention. The Career-Minded majority represents the continuity in our society. On virtually every count, they hold the more traditional values on family, marriage, work, religion, saving for the future, morals, patriotism, authority, and property. It is the other group of students, the 39 per cent minority, who are the devotees of the new values. Here is where we see the erosion of the Puritan Ethic in its clearest form and the impatience with all forms of authority and restraints—one of the most familiar hallmarks of the campus rebellion. We see also new attitudes toward nature, new forms of experimentation with marriage and communal living, the devaluation of money and success, and the great stress on self-expression and self-realization.

This latter group of students has also expressed the most passionate interest in changing the society, and has consistently held the most critical views of our social and political institutions. They played the pivotal role in the wave of campus strikes in 1968, 1969, and 1970, particularly on Ivy League campuses where they often formed a majority. Campus authorities were prepared to cope with the small number of campus activists. They were not prepared for the massive student support that came mainly from the Affluence-for-Granted camp. If campuses were quieter in 1971, the cause rested not with any serious reduction in activist numbers or passions. Rather, it was student support that was lacking—support that in the past had been supplied mainly by this large Affluence-for-Granted group.

When the Yankelovich organization first recognized the existence of this group in the mid-1960's, they were referred to as "Post-Affluents." However, in the 1968 study for *Fortune*, the editors labeled them "Forerunners," on the grounds that the taking of affluence for granted, and acceptance of the values that go with that assumption, are precursors of future shifts in values among the population at large. We believe this interpretation to be correct—up to a

94

point. The values held by the so-called Forerunner group *are* slowly spreading to others in the population, including the more Career-Minded majority of college students. The present study provides ample documentation of how these values are gradually making their way into the mainstream of student opinion. On the other hand, to the extent that these Forerunner values are tied to affluence, they will spread only if affluence itself spreads—a sound possibility, but, unfortunately, by no means a certainty. Also, the label Forerunner bears a heavier freight of judgment and interpretation than is proper in descriptive research. So, with this present study, we drop the Forerunner term and revert to more awkward but less judgmental designations.

In what follows we present a brief description of how these two groups of students—the Career-Minded and those who take affluence for granted—differ from each other, followed by a series of summary tables that present a detailed picture of similarities and differences.

Demographic Characteristics

The first fact of interest to be noted about these two groups is that there are so few objective demographic differences between them. Men and women students are equally represented in each of the two groups—roughly 50–50. The Career-Minded group is slightly skewed toward families with a lower education level: 46% of the Career-Minded students have fathers who have not attended college, compared with 41 per cent of the Affluence-for-Granted students. However, even this slight difference evaporates when we look at the father's occupation. Each of the two groups has exactly the same proportion of fathers in the professional, managerial, and white collar categories and in the blue collar occupations. Whites and non-whites are proportionately represented, and each group contains the same number of students who work part or full time.

There are, however, large differences between the two as to their college majors. The Career-Minded group contains many more science, engineering, and business majors (42% to 25%), and conversely, there are more humanities, social science, and education majors in the Post-Affluent group (63% to 51%). This latter group, however, has less of a predominantly humanities/social science complexion than it did several years ago. It now has drawn into it more science, engineering, and business majors.

Mood Profile

The campus change of mood from last year has affected both the Career-Minded and the Affluence-for-Granted groups in approximately the same way, with some subtle shadings of difference. Both report that they are more involved in their own private lives and happier than they were last year. But the Career-Minded are more satisfied with their present life and more serious about studying. The major difference in mood between the two groups is in relation to political issues. The Affluence-for-Granted camp reports itself as being more discouraged than the Career-Minded majority, more cynical, more doubtful of the chance to change society, less sure of the country's health, and more skeptical of the honesty of our political leaders.

Social and Personal Values

On values relating to war and peace, Career-Minded students are readier, by a 2-to-1 margin, to resort to warfare as an instrument of policy. The differences are particularly sharp with respect to wars designed to protect our national interest, contain Communists, maintain our position of power in the world, and fight for our honor. Moreover, this 2-to-1 ratio has remained constant each year—1968, 1969, 1970, and 1971.

With regard to social restraints, both groups accept the prohibition against heroin, but this is the only attitude toward authority they share in common. Once again, by almost 2-to-1 margins, the Affluence-for-Granted group finds it far more difficult than the majority to accept the power and authority of the police, the prohibition against marijuana, the authority of a boss in work, settling down to a routine, keeping one's views to oneself, and abiding by laws one may not agree with. Here, also, the same ratios between the two groups have held relatively constant over the series of four studies.

Career-Minded students, to a far greater extent than their Post-Affluent peers, condemn as morally wrong destroying private property, collecting welfare when one could work, paying one's way through college by selling dope, extramarital sex relations, leaving the country to avoid the draft, and homosexuality between consenting partners. Interestingly, however, the same *rank order* of moral prohibitions prevails for each of the two groups.

There is a more than 20 percentage point spread between the two groups on feelings about the sacredness of private property, the belief that competition encourages excellence, and the desire for more emphasis on law and order, the more traditional allegiance in each instance belonging to the Career-Minded majority. There is a spread of 10 to 20 percentage points between the two groups on an even wider range of values, including the beliefs that business is entitled to a profit, that hard work will always pay off, that one should save in order to avoid depending on others, that children should respect their parents, and that a legally based authority is needed to avoid chaos in the society. The more traditional and conservative beliefs are prevalent among the Career-Minded. The Affluence-for-Granted group, on the other hand, places more emphasis on creativity, being close to nature, self-expression and sexual freedom, and less emphasis on money, technology, family, religion, patriotism, and comfort.

The Affluence-for-Granted camp is less marriage-prone, less interested in having children, and a great deal more interested in living in communes or off the land.

In choosing careers, self-expression and the opportunity to make a contribution are more important to the Affluence-for-Granteds, and job security, the chance to get ahead, money, and prestige are less important by a 2-to-1 ratio. Interestingly, some doubts about being able to make as much money as they might like have crept into the thinking of the Affluence-for-Granted group, and money has become a relatively more important career consideration for them than in the past.

It is only on those intensely personal values the individual deems to be very important to his life that a somewhat different pattern prevails. Here, in many instances, there are no differences, or only minor ones, between the two groups. This parity on important personal values holds true for: love, friendship, education, privacy, doing things for others, and beauty.

Political Values

On political values, the Career-Minded students are consistently more moderate or conservative than the Affluence-for-Granted students. We single out for attention only the most glaring differences.

By wide margins, the Post-Affluents are far more likely than the Career-Mindeds to believe:

—The country has become a "sick society"
—Radical change is needed
—Radicals and blacks cannot be assured of a fair trial
—Women are an oppressed group
—Big business, the political parties, and the FBI stand in need of fundamental reform
—A new political party should be organized
—One should work with the protest movement in preference to the Establishment
—Tactics such as sit-ins, destroying draft board records, and shielding political prisoners can always be justified

On all of these and many other issues the Affluence-for-Granted students assume more radical positions by virtually 2-to-1 margins over the Career-Minded majority. Conversely, the belief that the police should not hesitate to use force, confidence in creating respect for law and order as a method for creating social change, and confidence in working with business leaders within the Establishment are all characteristic attitudes of the Career-Minded students. The Career-Mindeds are also more likely to believe that no one was responsible at My Lai and to justify "using people as tools," if the purpose is morally justified.

We see here the presence of fundamentally different orientations toward life. Whether or not these are caused by differing attitudes toward affluence—or whether the psychology of affluence is in itself a reflection of more fundamental forces—cannot be answered here. But at the very least we do know that taking affluence for granted is correlated with a broad range of new personal, social, cultural, and political values.

Tables 51 through 54 that follow present profiles of the demographic mood, cultural values, and political values of Career-Minded students compared to Affluence-for-Granted students.

Table **51.**   Demographic Profile According to Career-Minded vs. Post-Affluent Values

	1971		1970		1969		1968	
	Career Minded	Post-Affluent Values	Career Minded	Post-Affluent Values	Career Minded	Post-Affluent Values	Career Minded	Post-Affluent Values
	%	%	%	%	%	%	%	%
Sex								
Male	50	52	51	45	61	49	67	55
Female	50	48	49	55	39	51	33	45
Age								
Under 21 years	55	58	59	66	68	65	49	53
21 years and older	45	42	41	34	32	35	51	47
Father's education								
High school or less	46	41	*	*	*	*	*	*
Some college	21	22	*	*	*	*	*	*
College graduate/post-graduate	33	37	*	*	*	*	*	*
Father's occupation								
Professional/managerial and white collar	67	68	65	71	63	68	56	69
Blue collar	18	19	25	17	26	24	33	26
Other	15	13	10	12	11	8	11	5
Race								
White	87	87	87	92	92	94	93	94
Non-white	13	13	13	8	8	6	7	6

Major

Humanities/social science and education	51	63	45	68	*	*	46	80
Science/engineering/business	42	25	39	22	*	*	54	20
Undecided and other	7	12	16	10	*	*	*	*
Religion								
Protestant	43	31	46	33	53	43	*	*
Catholic	24	17	18	12	27	21	*	*
Jewish	10	8	8	12	9	12	*	*
Other and none	23	44	28	43	11	24	*	*
Employment								
Working part time/full time	49	49	*	*	47	50	47	38
Not working	51	51	*	*	53	50	53	62
Region								
Northeast	22	28	17	39	20	26	26	27
North Central	27	27	32	28	36	30	29	27
South	25	22	33	22	32	19	27	20
West	26	23	18	11	22	25	18	26

* Question was not asked.

101

Table 52. Mood Profile According to Career-Minded vs. Post-Affluent Values

	1971 Career Minded %	1971 Post-Affluent Values %	1970 Career Minded %	1970 Post-Affluent Values %	1969 Career Minded %	1969 Post-Affluent Values %	1968 Career Minded %	1968 Post-Affluent Values %
Change of mood since last year								
More involved in private life	62	59	*	*	*	*	*	*
Happier in personal life	55	55	*	*	*	*	*	*
More serious about studying	51	44	*	*	*	*	*	*
More fearful of future job chances	51	48	*	*	*	*	*	*
More doubtful of chance to change society	26	36	*	*	*	*	*	*
More determined to do something	25	30	*	*	*	*	*	*
More feeling of individual powerlessness	28	31	*	*	*	*	*	*
More doubtful of political leaders' honesty	48	58	*	*	*	*	*	*
Less accepting of violence	47	39	*	*	*	*	*	*
Less alienated	37	28	*	*	*	*	*	*
Less politically conservative	36	51	*	*	*	*	*	*
Less sure of country's health	37	49	*	*	*	*	*	*

Current mood

Confused about the future	54	56	*	*	*	*	*
Happy	54	43	*	*	*	*	*
Skeptical	29	31	*	*	*	*	*
Involved	26	30	*	*	*	*	*
Frustrated	25	32	*	*	*	*	*
Satisfied	27	19	*	*	*	*	*
Discouraged	18	25	*	*	*	*	*
Cynical	11	20	*	*	*	*	*
Agitated	11	16	*	*	*	*	*

* Question was not asked.

Table 53. Political Profile According to Career-Minded vs. Post-Affluent Values

	1971		1970		1969		1968	
	Career Minded	Post-Affluent Values	Career Minded	Post-Affluent Values	Career Minded	Post-Affluent Values	Career Minded	Post-Affluent Values
	%	%	%	%	%	%	%	%
Country is faring pretty badly/very badly	56	71	*	*	*	*	*	*
Believe the war will be over by 1972 election	13	12	*	*	*	*	*	*
Believe the economy will improve this year	30	20	*	*	*	*	*	*
Agree that country is a "sick society"	▲38	57	*	*	*	*	▲32	50
Believe that radical change is needed/system ought to be replaced	17	42	*	*	*	*	*	*
Real power in the country vested in giant corporations/financial institutions	52	67	*	*	*	*	*	*
System not democratic—the special interests propagandize the mass of people	50	69	*	*	*	*	*	*

Agree strongly or partially that:

Business too concerned with profits ... not enough with public responsibility

sibility	91	96	93	98	93	94	*	*
Economic well-being unjustly and unfairly distributed	77	88	85	94	77	91	*	*
We are a racist nation	78	86	87	92	76	80	*	*
Our two-party system offers no real alternative	69	79	79	91	*	*	*	*
People's privacy is being destroyed	79	87	*	*	*	*	*	*
Police should not hesitate to use force	▲62	41	*	*	*	*	*	*
Minority must not impose its will on the majority	51	53	*	*	65	60	*	*
Too much concern for welfare bum, not enough for person struggling to make a living	75	60		*	78	57	*	*
Groups that cannot be assured a fair trial								
Black Panthers	59	74	64	83	*	*	*	*
Radicals	43	58	53	71	*	*	*	*
Drug addicts	40	55	45	58	*	*	*	*
Middle-class blacks	▲23	▲38	36	48	*	*	*	*
Indians	32	52	43	58	*	*	*	*
Manufacturers of defective products	15	23	12	17	*	*	*	*
Polluters	23	29	*	*	*	*	*	*

(Continued on next page)

105

	1971		1970		1969		1968	
	Career Minded	Post-Affluent Values	Career Minded	Post-Affluent Values	Career Minded	Post-Affluent Values	Career Minded	Post-Affluent Values
	%	%	%	%	%	%	%	%
Groups that are oppressed								
Blacks	77	88	*	*	*	*	*	*
Women	26	45	*	*	*	*	*	*
College students	23	35	*	*	*	*	*	*
Homosexuals	84	84	*	*	*	*	*	*
Needs fundamental reform or should be done away with								
Big business	35	63	40	68	24	52	*	*
The military	62	77	66	82	53	71	*	*
The trade unions	39	39	48	50	41	43	*	*
The political parties	46	64	62	75	50	66	*	*
The FBI	30	54	21	45	*	*	*	*
The Supreme Court	19	30	31	35	*	*	*	*
The Constitution	13	25	14	18	*	*	*	*
Best method for creating social change								
Individual working in his own community	76	80	*	*	*	*	*	*
Changing the outlook of the public ..	50	64	*	*	*	*	*	*
Create respect for law and order ..	50	27	*	*	*	*	*	*
Organize new political party	21	32	*	*	*	*	*	*

	Col 1	Col 2	Col 3	Col 4	Col 5	Col 6	Col 7	Col 8
Nationalize private industry	11	21	*	*	*	*	*	*
Create conditions for revolution	7	17	*	*	*	*	*	*
Prefer to work with protest movement rather than with the Establishment	14	▶27	18	18	*	*	*	*
Within establishment prefer to work with:								
Community leaders	43	39	40	39	*	*	*	*
Business leaders	22	13	18	12	*	*	*	*
Federal agencies	15	14	18	7	*	*	*	*
Candidates for political office	12	13	6	11	*	*	*	*
Unqualifiedly opposed to violence	60	51	*	*	*	*	*	*
Tactics that are always justified								
Sit-ins	19	35	17	30	6	18	*	*
Blockade of buildings	3	9	2	6	2	2	*	*
Assaulting police	1	7	1	2	1	*	*	*
Destroying draft board records	4	16	3	10	*	*	*	*
Shielding political prisoners	8	20	*	*	*	*	*	*
Using people as tools if purpose is morally justified	38	27	*	*	*	*	*	*
My Lai								
We are all responsible	37	46	*	*	*	*	*	*
No one is responsible	33	18	*	*	*	*	*	*

* Question was not asked.

Table 54. Social and Personal Values Profile According to Career-Minded vs. Post-Affluent Values

	1971		1970		1969		1968	
	Career Minded	Post-Affluent Values	Career Minded	Post-Affluent Values	Career Minded	Post-Affluent Values	Career Minded	Post-Affluent Values
	%	%	%	%	%	%	%	%
Values worth fighting a war for								
Counteracting aggression	55	41	60	35	64	47	75	50
Protecting our national interests	37	20	37	20	51	25	65	40
Containing the Communists	36	18	41	17	55	31	59	28
Maintaining our position of power in the world	24	11	20	11	33	17	46	22
Fighting for our honor	23	11	21	12	33	15	44	20
Keeping a commitment	16	10	14	14	17	12	24	14
Social restraints that are easily acceptable								
Prohibition against heroin	86	79	88	83	*	*	*	*
Power and authority of police	54	31	54	31	58	38	72	44
Prohibition against marijuana	50	31	59	30	59	35	69	37
Authority of a "boss" in work	45	23	50	29	56	40	60	52
Settling down to a routine	31	19	*	*	*	*	*	*
Keeping your views to yourself	19	10	*	*	*	*	*	*
Abiding by laws you don't agree with	17	8	21	12	17	12	35	21
Seen as morally wrong								
Taking things without paying for them	83	72	*	*	*	*	*	*

	*	*	*	*	*	*	*
	*	*	*	*	*	*	*
	*	*	*	*	*	68	*
Destroying private property	79	62	*	*	*	*	*
Collecting welfare when you could work	81	65	*	*	*	*	*
Paying one's way through college by selling dope	70	52	*	*	*	*	*
Extramarital sex relations	62	49	*	*	84	68	*
Having children without marriage ..	49	30	*	*	*	*	*
Leaving the country to avoid the draft	35	18	*	*	*	*	*
Homosexuals	32	16	*	*	52	29	*
Casual sex relations	28	19	*	*	*	*	*
Very important personal values							
Love	87	87	*	*	82	88	*
Friendship	86	87	*	*	85	86	*
Education	76	72	*	*	80	79	*
Privacy	67	61	*	*	62	60	*
Family	70	57	*	*	*	*	*
Doing things for others	59	59	*	*	45	57	*
Creativity	46	61	*	*	*	*	*
Being close to nature	43	53	*	*	*	*	*
Comfort	47	31	*	*	*	*	*
Living a clean moral life	35	31	*	*	50	39	*
Religion	34	26	*	*	40	36	*
Nationalism	33	18	*	*	41	29	*
Money	21	12	*	*	26	8	*
Beauty	19	19	*	*	*	*	*

(Continued on next page)

	1968		1969		1970		1971	
	Career Minded %	Post-Affluent Values %	Career Minded %	Post-Affluent Values %	Career Minded %	Post-Affluent Values %	Career Minded %	Post-Affluent Values %
Extent of belief in traditional values								
Business is entitled to a profit	*	*	*	*	*	*	92	73
Need for legally based authority	*	*	95	89	*	*	90	79
Children should respect parents	*	*	*	*	*	*	92	79
Importance of a meaningful career	*	*	*	*	*	*	82	73
Accept the legal consequences of breaking the law	*	*	*	*	*	*	74	63
Sacredness of private property	*	*	82	66	*	*	79	55
Competition encourages excellence	*	*	83	60	*	*	71	48
Saving to avoid dependency on others	65	51	84	65	*	*	73	59
Hard work will always pay off	78	58	64	47	*	*	44	31
Welcome changes in values								
More emphasis on self-expression	68	90	78	91	*	*	76	87
Less emphasis on money	53	80	63	82	*	*	71	84
More acceptance of sexual freedom	*	*	37	52	*	*	51	63
More emphasis on law and order	78	39	*	*	*	*	60	35
More emphasis on technology	*	*	66	43	*	*	45	29
Less difference between the sexes	*	*	*	*	*	*	30	41
Marriage								
Agree that marriage is obsolete	*	*	20	28	25	34	28	42
Look forward to being legally married	*	*	*	*	*	*	69	48
Interested in having children	*	*	*	*	*	*	83	73

110

Living off the land has appeal (permanently/year or two)	35	54	*	*	*	*	*	*
Career choice								
Have no doubt about being able to make as much money as I want ..	48	52	57	71	52	68	*	*
Have no doubt about being as successful as I want	65	62	*	*	68	67	*	*
Factors important in career choice								
Make a contribution	67	74	68	82	70	83	71	80
Challenge of the job	66	67	64	63	72	71	77	74
Self-expression	56	75	48	71	57	77	63	75
Job security	56	29	38	25	53	31	*	*
Chance to get ahead	45	19	*	*	*	*	*	*
Money	54	29	46	19	57	23	58	21
Prestige	28	14	18	10	30	15	33	13
Barriers to getting a desirable job								
Unwillingness to conform	17	35	*	*	*	*	*	*
Political views	9	25	*	*	*	*	*	*
Race	11	11	*	*	*	*	*	*

* Question was not asked.

111

CHAPTER 8

The New Left

FOR A SMALL MINORITY GROUP on campus, the New Left has received a disproportionate share of attention from both the mass media and the adult world.

Using as broad a definition as "identification" rather than membership, activity, or even ideological commitment, still only one out of ten students can currently be classified as New Left.

Also there has been remarkably little shift in the size of the New Left campus core over the past few years. In 1969, about 13 per cent of the students[1] claimed to identify with the New Left; 14 per cent in 1970,[2] and 11 per cent in 1971. At best, what has occurred has been a replacement of the cadre which dropped out, graduated from college, or left the "movement"—but with no real expansion or contraction taking place in the overall size of the group.

From the outset of the current student rebellion, there has been an unconscious tendency on the part of many to obfuscate or blur the differences between the New Left and the Take-Affluence-for-Granted groups who share some of the same life-style values and attitudes, but not the same political ideology. As the results of this study indicate, the New Left has never been as sizable, nor the Post-Affluent sector as radical, as many people thought.

The qualities that distinguish the New Left, and set it apart from the broader Post-Affluent base of college students include:

---

[1] *Generations Apart*. CBS News, 1969.

[2] *Youth and the Establishment*. JDR 3rd Fund, 1971.

—Deeper commitment to radicalism;

—The search for political ideology;

—The adoption of the counterculture as a tactic and tool of revolutionary change rather than just a new life style and value system;

—Greater willingness to use whatever tools and tactics are necessary, from violence to manipulation, for the sake of the "cause";

—A Marxian view of society and its institutions;

—A deep-seated sense of alienation; partly self-imposed, partly cherished.

Seven out of ten New Left students (72%) believe that their personal values are *not* shared by most Americans. Eight out of ten (77%) find it extremely difficult or intolerable to accept the idea of living a "conventional" life. Six out of ten (59%) would prefer to live in another country or society.

Other characteristics, values, and attitudes which set the New Left as a group apart from other students on the campus, including the more liberal Affluence-for-Granted sector, embrace the following:

Demographic Characteristics

Despite the fact that the New Left is more committed to women's liberation than other students, it is still the most male-dominated group. In the New Left, 69 per cent are men, 31 per cent women. This compares with the almost even split for the total student population (51% men; 49% women) and for the Affluence-for-Granted sector (52% men; 48% women).

While coming from the same upper-middle-class background as the Post-Affluents, the New Left student tends to be somewhat older (49% are 21 years of age or older); more likely to come from the Northeast (40% New Left; 28% Affluence-for-Granted); more apt to be studying the humanities (56% to 48%). A greater percentage of the New Left is either Jewish (18%) or with no religious identification (53%) than is true for the Post-Affluents. Among the latter, 8 per cent are Jewish, 44 per cent have no religious identification.

113

Mood Profile

The general campus mood in the spring of 1971 affected the New Left, but with somewhat different results.

Compared to the previous year, the New Left is considerably more frustrated, more cynical, more radical in its views, and unlike other students, more involved.

The sharpest differences in the moods of the New Left and Affluence-for-Granted students compared to the previous year include:

—More feeling of individual powerlessness (41%, New Left; 31%, Affluence-for-Granted).
—More doubtful of political leaders' honesty (67%, New Left; 58% Affluence-for-Granted).
—Less politically conservative (72% to 51%).
—Less sure of the country's health (59% to 49%).

There are also noticeable differences in the current moods of the two groups. Compared to the Post-Affluent students, the New Left is:

—More involved (44% to 30%)
—More frustrated (40% to 32%)
—More cynical (36% to 20%)
—More agitated (24% to 16%)
—Less confused about the future (47% to 56%)

Political Values

Marxian underpinnings dominate the political thinking of the New Left. Compared to the Post-Affluent students, those who identify with the New Left feel far more strongly that:

—The real power in the country is vested in the giant corporations and financial institutions (82%, New Left; 67%, Post-Affluents).
—Radical change is needed and the system ought to be replaced (65%, New Left; 42%, Post-Affluents).
—Economic well-being is unjustly and unfairly distributed (99%, New Left; 88%, Post-Affluents).

114

—Seventy-three per cent of the New Left agree that "We are a sick society," compared to 57 per cent of the Post-Affluents.

Another distinguishing mark of the New Left is their attitude toward violence. Only 25 per cent believe that the police should not hesitate to use force compared to 41 per cent of the Post-Affluent students and 62 per cent of the Career-Minded. Similarly only a third of the New Left (33%) are unqualifiedly opposed to violence in comparison with 51 per cent of the Post-Affluents and 60 per cent of the Career-Minded.

The feelings of the New Left on tactics reiterate the same pattern:

Among the New Left, 56 per cent feel that sit-ins are always justified compared to 35 per cent of the Post-Affluents; on blockades, the figures are 21 per cent to 9 per cent; on draft boards, 34 per cent to 16 per cent; on shielding political prisoners, 40 per cent to 20 per cent.

Social justice—or the absence of it—is the special flag and banner of the New Left. Here it is a difference of emphasis and moral indignation that distinguishes the New Left from the Affluence-for-Granted students. Significant examples of this include the belief that:

—Black Panthers cannot get a fair trial (93% New Left; 74% Post-Affluent)
—Nor can radicals (76% New Left; 58% Post-Affluents)
—Nor Indians (69% New Left; 52% Post-Affluents)

It is also the New Left students who are far more convinced that women are oppressed in the United States (61%) than Post-Affluents (45%).

Large majorities of the New Left also believe that major institutions in our society—big business, the military, the political parties, and the FBI—need fundamental reform or should be done away with.

Yet despite the New Left's radical diagnosis of society, acceptance of violence, attitudes toward institutions, and feelings about social justice, there is a curious confusion and ambivalence about how to bring about desired social change.

Surprisingly, three out of four of the New Left still believe that the best methods for creating social change are working in communities and changing the outlook of the public. Compared to the Post-Affluents, only 12 per cent more of the New Left call for organizing a new political party (44%); only 19 per cent more want to see private industry nationalized (40%); and only 18 per cent more want to create conditions for revolution (35%).

Social and Political Values

On war, the New Left, even more than the Post-Affluents, categorically reject the values of the war. Similarly they find social restraints far less acceptable. Only 9 per cent of the New Left can easily accept the power and authority of the police compared to 31 per cent of the Post-Affluents; only 12 per cent can accept the prohibition against marijuana compared to 31 per cent of the Post-Affluents; only 13 per cent can accept the authority of a boss; 12 per cent, settling down to a routine; 3 per cent, abiding by laws one doesn't agree with.

Where the New Left and the Post-Affluents part company most sharply is on the subject of what is morally wrong.

Differences of close to 20 percentage points separate the New Left and Post-Affluents on the morality of:

—Taking things without paying for them,
—Destroying private property,
—Collecting welfare when you could work,
—Paying one's way through college by selling dope.

Very Important Personal Values

It is in the area of important and very personal values that the New Left and the Post-Affluents come very close together. Both groups share similar feelings about the importance of love, friendship, education, privacy, creativity, and being close to nature.

The feelings of the two groups about career choice and factors important in deciding on a career are strikingly parallel. The one significant difference in this area is that 50 per cent of the New Left see lack of "willingness to conform" as a major barrier to getting a desirable job compared to 35 per cent of the Post-Affluents.

116

In personal values and life style, however, the major differences between the New Left and the Post-Affluents include attitudes toward family and the more extreme views of the former students on sexual freedom.

Only 39 per cent of the New Left consider family a very important personal value compared to 57 per cent of the Post-Affluents.

—On sexual freedom, 87 per cent of the New Left would welcome more acceptance compared to 63 per cent of Post-Affluents.
—Sixty per cent of the New Left agree that marriage is obsolete. (Only 42 per cent of the Post-Affluents share this view.)
—Twenty-nine per cent consider extramarital sex relations as morally wrong compared to almost half of the Post-Affluents (49%).
—Only 10 per cent see having children without marriage as morally wrong, in contrast to 30 per cent of the Post-Affluents who feel the same way.

These and other findings on the New Left are included in Tables 55 through 58.

Table **55.**   Demographic Profile According to Special Segments

	Total	New Left	Post-Affluent Values	Career Minded
	%	%	%	%
Sex				
Male	51	69	52	50
Female	49	31	48	50
Age				
Under 21 years	56	51	58	55
21 years and older	44	49	42	45
Father's education				
High school or less	44	41	41	46
Some college	21	21	22	21
College graduate/post-graduate	35	38	37	33

(Continued on next page)

117

	Total	New Left	Post-Affluent Values	Career Minded
	%	%	%	%
Father's occupation				
Professional/managerial	49	49	49	49
White collar	18	19	19	18
Blue collar	19	22	19	18
Other	14	10	13	15
Race				
White	87	83	87	87
Non-white	13	17	13	13
Major				
Humanities/social science	38	56	48	32
Education	18	7	15	19
Science/engineering/business	35	23	25	42
Undecided/other	9	14	12	7
Religion				
Protestant	39	17	31	43
Catholic	21	12	17	24
Jewish	9	18	8	10
Other/none	31	53	44	23
Employment				
Working part time/full time	49	41	49	49
Not working	51	59	51	51
Region				
Northeast	24	40	28	22
North Central	27	18	27	27
South	24	13	22	25
West	25	29	23	26

118

Table **56.**   Mood Profile According to Special Segments

	Total	New Left	Post-Affluent Values	Career Minded
	%	%	%	%
Change of mood since last year				
More involved in private life	61	55	59	62
Happier in personal life	55	53	55	55
More serious about studying	48	43	44	51
More fearful of future job chances ...	50	46	48	51
More doubtful of chance to change society	30	40	36	26
More determined to do something ...	27	36	30	25
More feeling of individual powerlessness	29	41	31	28
More doubtful of political leaders' honesty	52	67	58	48
Less accepting of violence	44	26	39	47
Less alienated	33	24	28	37
Less politically conservative	41	72	51	36
Less sure of country's health	42	59	49	37
Current mood				
Confused about the future	55	47	56	54
Happy	50	39	43	54
Skeptical	30	36	31	29
Involved	28	44	30	26
Frustrated	27	40	32	25
Satisfied	24	16	19	27
Discouraged	21	33	25	18
Cynical	15	36	20	11
Agitated	13	24	16	11

119

Table **57.** Political Profile According to Special Segments

	Total	New Left	Post-Affluent Values	Career Minded
	%	%	%	%
Country is faring pretty badly/very badly	62	82	71	56
Believe the war will be over by 1972 election	13	12	12	13
Believe the economy will improve this year	26	17	20	30
Agree that country is a "sick society" ..	45	73	57	38
Believe that radical change is needed/ system ought to be replaced	27	65	42	17
Real power in the country vested in giant corporations/financial institutions ..	58	82	67	52
System not democratic—the special interests propagandize the mass of people	57	88	69	50
Agree strongly or partially that: Business too concerned with profits . . . not enough with public responsibility	93	100	96	91
Economic well-being unjustly and unfairly distributed	81	99	88	77
We are a racist nation	80	93	86	78
Our two-party system offers no real alternative	73	89	79	69
People's privacy is being destroyed ..	83	93	87	79
Police should not hesitate to use force	53	25	41	62
Minority must not impose its will on the majority	52	50	53	51
Too much concern for welfare bum, not enough for person struggling to make a living	68	44	60	75
Radicals of the Left are as much a threat as radicals of the Right	87	63	81	90

(Continued on next page)

	Total	New Left	Post-Affluent Values	Career Minded
	%	%	%	%
Groups that cannot be assured a fair trial				
Black Panthers	65	93	74	59
Radicals	49	76	58	43
Drug addicts	46	71	55	40
Middle-class blacks	29	54	38	23
Indians	40	69	52	32
Manufacturers of defective products	18	26	23	15
Polluters	25	31	29	23
Groups that are oppressed				
Blacks	81	93	88	77
Women	33	61	45	26
College students	27	46	35	23
Homosexuals	84	89	84	84
Needs fundamental reform or should be done away with				
Big business	46	75	63	35
The military	67	95	77	62
The trade unions	39	43	39	39
The political parties	54	79	64	46
The FBI	39	76	54	30
The Supreme Court	24	26	30	19
The Constitution	18	34	25	13
Best method for creating social change				
Individual working in his own community	78	77	80	76
Changing the outlook of the public	55	77	64	50
Create respect for law and order	41	10	27	50
Organize new political party	25	44	32	21
Nationalize private industry	15	40	21	11
Create conditions for revolution	11	35	17	7
Prefer to work with protest movement rather than with the Establishment	19	52	27	14

(Continued on next page)

121

	Total	New Left	Post-Affluent Values	Career Minded
	%	%	%	%
Within establishment prefer to work with:				
Community leaders	41	30	39	43
Business leaders	18	10	13	22
Federal agencies	15	14	14	15
Candidates for political office	12	17	13	12
Unqualifiedly opposed to violence	56	33	51	60
Tactics that are always justified				
Sit-ins	26	56	35	19
Blockade of buildings	5	21	9	3
Assaulting police	4	19	7	1
Destroying draft board records	9	34	16	4
Shielding political prisoners	13	40	20	8
Using people as tools if purpose is morally justified	34	36	27	38
My Lai				
We are all responsible	40	36	46	37
No one is responsible	27	10	18	33

Table **58.**   Social and Personal Values Profile According to Special Segments

	Total	New Left	Post-Affluent Values	Career Minded
	%	%	%	%
Values worth fighting a war for				
Counteracting aggression	50	27	41	55
Protecting our national interests	30	14	20	37
Containing the Communists	29	7	18	36
Maintaining our position of power in the world	19	4	11	24
Fighting for our honor	18	8	11	23
Keeping a commitment	14	6	10	16

(Continued on next page)

	Total	New Left	Post-Affluent Values	Career Minded
	%	%	%	%
Social restraints that are easily acceptable				
Prohibition against heroin	83	69	79	86
Power and authority of police	45	9	31	54
Prohibition against marijuana	42•	12	31	50
Authority of a "boss" in work	36	13	23	45
Settling down to a routine	26	12	19	31
Keeping your views to yourself	16	5	10	19
Abiding by laws you don't agree with	13	3	8	17
Seen as morally wrong				
Taking things without paying for them	78	56	72	83
Destroying private property	72	44	62	79
Collecting welfare when you could work	75	43	65	81
Paying one's way through college by selling dope	63	27	52	70
Extramarital sex relations	57	29	49	62
Having children without marriage	42	10	30	49
Leaving the country to avoid the draft	28	4	18	35
Homosexuality	26	7	16	32
Casual sex relations	25	6	19	28
Very important personal values				
Love	87	79	87	87
Friendship	87	86	87	86
Education	74	76	72	76
Privacy	64	59	61	67
Family	65	39	57	70
Doing things for others	59	48	59	59
Creativity	52	59	61	46
Being close to nature	47	53	53	43
Comfort	40	33	31	47
Living a clean moral life	34	14	31	35
Religion	31	12	26	34
Nationalism	27	9	18	33
Money	18	10	12	21
Beauty	19	22	19	19

(Continued on next page)

123

	Total	New Left	Post-Affluent Values	Career Minded
	%	%	%	%
Extent of belief in traditional values				
Business is entitled to a profit	85	59	73	92
Need for legally based authority	86	68	79	90
Children should respect parents	87	64	79	92
Importance of a meaningful career	79	62	73	82
Accept the legal consequences of breaking the law	70	42	63	74
Sacredness of private property	69	34	55	79
Competition encourages excellence ..	62	39	48	71
Saving to avoid dependency on others	67	50	59	73
Hard work will always pay off	39	20	31	44
Welcome changes in values				
More emphasis on self-expression ...		94	87	76
Less emphasis on money	76	90	84	71
More acceptance of sexual freedom ..	56	87	63	51
More emphasis on law and order	50	21	35	60
More emphasis on technology	39	30	29	45
Less difference between the sexes	34	61	41	30
Marriage				
Agree that marriage is obsolete	34	60	42	28
Look forward to being legally married	61	28	48	69
Interested in having children	79	60	73	83
Living off the land has appeal (permanently/year or two)	43	69	54	35
Career choice				
Have no doubts about being able to make as much money as I want to ..	50	50	52	48
Have no doubts about being as successful as I want to	64	58	62	65
Factors important in career choice				
Make a contribution	70	76	74	67
Challenge of the job	66	64	67	66
Self-expression	63	73	75	56
Job security	46	27	29	56
Chance to get ahead	35	21	19	45
Money	44	28	29	54
Prestige	22	16	14	28

(Continued on next page)

124

	Total	New Left	Post-Affluent Values	Career Minded
	%	%	%	%
Barriers to getting a desirable job				
Willingness to conform	24	50	35	17
Political views	15	48	25	9
Race	11	18	11	11
Self-identification				
Conservative/Moderate-Conservative .	21	3	12	26
Middle of the road	16	1	11	20
Liberal	53	51	57	51
Radical	10	44	20	3
Political party identification				
Democrat	36	40	34	37
Republican	21	1	15	25
Other/None	43	59	51	38
New Left identification				
New Left	11	100	19	5
Non-New Left	89	—	81	95
Psychology of affluence				
Career-Minded	61	30	—	100
Take-Affluence-for-Granted	39	70	100	—
Measure of alienation				
Personal values not shared by most Americans	32	72	47	23
Hard/intolerable to accept conventional life	33	77	53	20
Prefer to live in other country or society	30	59	35	28

125

CHAPTER 9

Republicans, Democrats, and Unaffiliated

POLITICALLY, there are three groups on campus. The single largest group is made up of those who classify themselves as "independents or unaffiliateds," 43 per cent.

The next largest group is the Young Democrats (36%) and the smallest group is the Young Republicans (21%).

There are, however, far more interesting differences than size of membership which distinguish the three groups from each other.

The Republicans are the most elite, conservative, and pro-Establishment. While their social backgrounds would certainly qualify them as part of the Take-Affluence-for-Granted group on campus, 72 per cent classify themselves as Career-Minded. Essentially, the young Republicans believe in the system, are strong on law and order—and yet at the same time are troubled by many of the same questions besetting other more liberal and radical students. Among young Republicans, 85 per cent agree that business is too concerned with profits and not enough with social responsibility; 70 per cent believe that economic well-being is unjustly and unfairly distributed and that we are a racist nation. They, too, question the value of war, except for counteracting aggression, which a majority (61%) believe is worthwhile. Similarly they are also part of the search for new values, with a majority welcoming more emphasis on self-expression and less emphasis on money. However, the young Republicans hold to the more traditional views on marriage, extramarital relations, and having children without being married. Overall, the young Republicans are a strange combination of the old and the new. It is only the contrast between their stands and those of some of their liberal friends that makes them seem strait-laced and more like traditional college students of earlier generations.

126

The Democrats on campus still show heavy traces of the traditional Democratic Party alliances. Compared to the Republicans or the Unaffiliated, the group contains larger numbers of students from blue-collar, Catholic, and minority-group backgrounds. Fifty-one per cent of the Young Democrats come from homes in which the father has high school or less education; 20 per cent come from blue collar homes; 17 per cent are non-white, a decided contrast to the 3 per cent non-white who are Republicans.

These young Democrats are also quite radical in their views of many of society's institutions, but the vast majority are committed to effecting change within the present social structure. One of the qualities that distinguishes them from the Unaffiliated students is evidence of a dim hope in the present political party system.

The Unaffiliated students are certainly not the least political, but definitely the most disengaged. Three out of four of the group categorize themselves as radical (17%) or liberal (55%). Forty per cent believe that their personal values are not shared by most Americans compared to similar views expressed by only 30 per cent of the Democrats and 21 per cent of the Republicans.

The Unaffiliated contain the largest number of students who consider this a sick society or think that the system is not democratic.

There are, indeed, distinct differences in the views of the three political groupings on the campus, but also many similar and shared ideas. The sharpest line of demarcation is between the Republicans on the one hand and the Democrats and Unaffiliated on the other— with the last two groups being more similar than different.

Demographic Differences

Young Republicans, as indicated, are usually middle-class. (56 per cent have fathers who are professionals or hold managerial positions; 42 per cent have fathers who are college graduates.) Ninety-seven per cent are white; 65 per cent are Protestant; 44 per cent (the largest group) are studying science, business, or engineering. Politically, 49 per cent classify themselves as conservative; 22 per cent as middle-of-the-road; 29 per cent as liberal. Seventy-two per cent identify themselves as Career-Minded; 28 per cent as Post-Affluent.

Among the Democrats, 51 per cent have fathers with high school education or less; 34 per cent are Protestant, 29 per cent Catholic, 13 per cent Jewish, and 24 per cent no identification. Seventeen per cent are non-white. Fifty-eight per cent are studying humanities, social science, or education.

The Unaffiliated come from economic backgrounds more similar to the young Republicans than to the Democrats. Thirty-seven per cent have college graduate fathers; 51 per cent have fathers who are employed as professionals or executives. Unlike the Republicans, the majority are either Jewish (10%) or without religious identification (43%). Among the Unaffiliated, 55 per cent consider themselves to be liberal, 17 per cent radical, 14 per cent middle-of-the-road and only 13 per cent conservative.

Political Profile

Democrats and the Unaffiliated share very similar feelings on how things are going in the country, the economy, the end of the war, and the state of our society. The Republicans seem more optimistic and hopeful when compared with those groups than if their views are examined on their own.

For example, twice as many of the young Republicans believe that the war will be over by the 1972 elections—but it is still only one out of five of the group who feels this way (20%).

Or on the economy, again twice as many of the Republicans as the Democrats or Unaffiliated believed it would improve in 1971—but still only 41 per cent of the group was that hopeful.

In outlook, one of the biggest differences between the Republicans and other two groups is their view of the system. A sizable majority of the Democrats (60%) and the Unaffiliated (67%) believe that the system is not democratic—and that special interests propagandize the mass of the people. By contrast, only a minority (34%) of the Republicans share this view.

Sizable majorities of all three groups agree strongly or partially that:

—Business is too concerned with profits
—Economic well-being is unjustly and unfairly distributed

—We are a racist nation

—People's privacy is being destroyed

—Radicals of the Left are as much a threat as radicals of the Right

To varying degrees, all three groups also agree that our two-party system offers no real alternative. Eighty-two per cent of the Unaffiliated share this view, 71 per cent of the Democrats and 58 per cent of the Republicans.

On the other hand, it is only a majority of the Republicans who believe that the police should not hesitate to use force (75%).

Social Justice and Oppressed Groups

Half or more of the Democrats, Republicans and Unaffiliated agree that Black Panthers cannot be assured a fair trial. A large majority of each group also agrees that blacks and homosexuals are oppressed. On most other counts, the views of the Republicans are divergent from the other groups.

For example, about one out of two of the Democrats and Unaffiliated believes that drug addicts can't get a fair trial; only 29 per cent of the Republicans feel that way. Over 40 per cent of the former groups also feel the same way about Indians. Among Republicans, only 28 per cent share this view.

Views on women as an oppressed group are less manifest among Republicans, with only 17 per cent considered by women to be an oppressed group. Among Democrats, the figure is 38 per cent; among the Unaffiliated, 37 per cent.

Institutions

Republicans are less critical of big business, the military, the political parties and the FBI and more critical of trade unions than either the Democrats or the Unaffiliated.

On political parties, 64 per cent of the Unaffiliated, 51 per cent of the Democrats, and 36 per cent of the Republicans believe they need fundamental reform or should be done away with.

129

Creating Social Change

Democrats, Republicans, and the Unaffiliated all agree that the best method for creating social change is for the individual to work in his own community. However, the majority of the Republicans (72%) place almost equal stress on creating respect for law and order—a view rejected by most Democrats and the Unaffiliateds.

Values Worth Fighting a War for

With one exception, the majority of students—regardless of political affiliation—reject war as a value worth fighting for. The one exception is the 61 per cent of the Republicans who believe that counteracting aggression is worth fighting for. Also, unlike Democrats and the Unaffiliated, the Republicans are more evenly divided on the value of fighting to protect our national interest or for the purpose of containing Communists.

Social Restraints

A majority of Republicans (41%), unlike Democrats and the Unaffiliated, find it easy to accept the power and authority of a boss, and are somewhat more inclined to accept the idea of settling down to a routine than Democrats (23%) or the Unaffiliated (21%).

Moral Positions

Republicans take the most traditionally moral position, the Democrats come next, and the Unaffiliated are last. A general example is the subject of taking things without paying for them. Among Republicans, 88 per cent see this as wrong; among Democrats, 81 per cent; the Unaffiliated, 71 per cent.

This same pattern is repeated in attitudes on the morality of extramarital sex, having children without marriage, and homosexuality.

Very Important Personal Values

The three groups of students look very similarly on love, friendship, education, privacy, doing things for others, comfort and beauty.

More Republicans than either Democrats or the Unaffiliated, however, place emphasis on religion, nationalism, and living a clean moral life, and money.

Compared to the Democrats, fewer of the Unaffiliated place as much value on family or religion.

Traditional Values

In varying degrees, the majority of the three political groups accept the traditional values—with one fascinating exception. A majority of the Republicans (53%) believe that hard work will always pay off. Only a minority of the Democrats (39%) or the Unaffiliated (33%) share this view. It is also interesting to note that what Republicans take into account in choosing a career is also different—with more emphasis placed on challenge of the job, security, advancement, and money—and less on self-expression.

These and other findings for the three political groups can be found in the tables which follow (Tables 59–62).

Table **59.** Demographic Profile According to Political Affiliation

	Total	Demo-crat	Repub-lican	Other/None
	%	%	%	%
Sex				
Male	51	50	50	52
Female	49	50	50	48
Age				
Under 21 years	56	54	54	58
21 years and older	44	46	46	42
Father's education				
High school or less	44	51	38	41
Some college	21	20	20	22
College graduate/post-graduate	35	29	42	37

(Continued on next page)

131

	Total	Demo-crat	Repub-lican	Other/None
	%	%	%	%
Father's occupation				
Professional/managerial	49	43	56	51
White collar	18	18	18	19
Blue collar	19	20	16	18
Other	14	19	10	12
Race				
White	87	83	97	87
Non-white	13	17	3	13
Major				
Humanities/social science	38	39	33	41
Education	18	19	18	15
Science/engineering/business	35	32	44	34
Undecided/other	9	10	5	10
Religion				
Protestant	39	34	65	28
Catholic	21	29	15	19
Jewish	9	13	2	10
Other/none	31	24	18	43
Employment				
Working part time/full time	49	50	50	47
Not working	51	50	50	53
Region				
Northeast	24	25	13	29
North Central	27	27	31	25
South	24	24	26	24
West	25	24	30	22

Table **60.**   Mood Profile According to Political Affiliation

	Total	Demo-crat	Repub-lican	Other/None
	%	%	%	%
Change of mood since last year				
More involved in private life	61	65	59	58
Happier in personal life	55	57	55	55
More serious about studying	48	49	50	47
More fearful of future job chances ...	50	53	47	49

(Continued on next page)

	Total	Demo-crat	Repub-lican	Other/None
	%	%	%	%
More doubtful of chance to change society	30	34	17	32
More determined to do something ...	27	27	22	29
More feeling of individual powerlessness	29	27	20	35
More doubtful of political leaders' honesty	52	53	37	59
Less accepting of violence	44	47	50	38
Less alienated	33	38	40	26
Less politically conservative	41	41	29	48
Less sure of country's health	42	42	30	46
Current mood				
Confused about the future	55	59	46	56
Happy	50	54	54	44
Skeptical	30	36	22	28
Involved	28	29	25	27
Frustrated	27	26	21	32
Satisfied	24	24	24	23
Discouraged	21	21	16	23
Cynical	15	16	8	16
Agitated	13	13	8	15

Table **61.** Political Profile According to Political Affiliation

	Total	Demo-crat	Repub-lican	Other/None
	%	%	%	%
Country is faring pretty badly/very badly	62	68	40	69
Believe the war will be over by 1972 election	13	11	20	10
Believe the economy will improve this year	26	22	41	22
Agree that country is a "sick society" ..	45	48	28	52
Believe that radical change is needed/system ought to be replaced	27	27	7	36

(Continued on next page)

	Total	Demo-crat	Repub-lican	Other/None
	%	%	%	%
Real power in the country vested in giant corporations/financial institutions	58	58	50	62
System not democratic—the special interests propagandize the mass of people	57	60	34	67
Agree strongly or partially that:				
Business too concerned with profits . . . not enough with public responsibility	93	95	85	94
Economic well-being unjustly and unfairly distributed	81	87	70	83
We are a racist nation	80	84	70	84
Our two-party system offers no real alternative	73	71	58	82
People's privacy is being destroyed	83	83	73	86
Police should not hesitate to use force	53	48	75	47
Minority must not impose its will on the majority	52	48	57	53
Too much concern for welfare bum, not enough for person struggling to make a living	68	61	85	67
Radicals of the Left are as much a threat as radicals of the Right	87	88	90	85
Groups that cannot be assured a fair trial				
Black Panthers	65	69	50	69
Radicals	49	52	33	55
Drug addicts	46	51	29	50
Middle-class blacks	29	29	19	33
Indians	40	41	28	44
Manufacturers of defective products	18	18	14	21
Polluters	25	24	23	28
Groups that are oppressed				
Blacks	81	86	68	83
Women	33	38	17	37
College students	27	28	22	29
Homosexuals	84	87	76	85

(Continued on next page)

134

	Total	Democrat	Republican	Other/None
	%	%	%	%
Needs fundamental reform or should be be done away with				
Big business	46	48	24	53
The military	67	70	49	76
The trade unions	39	36	47	38
The political parties	54	51	36	64
The FBI	39	42	19	47
The Supreme Court	24	21	23	26
The Constitution	18	16	8	25
Best method for creating social change				
Individual working in his own community	78	79	80	75
Changing the outlook of the public	55	58	49	56
Create respect for law and order	41	35	72	31
Organize new political party	25	27	13	29
Nationalize private industry	15	15	6	19
Create conditions for revolution	11	11	4	14
Prefer to work with protest movement rather than with the Establishment	19	22	4	24
Within the Establishment prefer to work with:				
Community leaders	41	41	48	38
Business leaders	18	14	25	19
Federal agencies	15	15	19	12
Candidates for political office	12	16	7	12
Unqualifiedly opposed to violence	56	56	62	53
Tactics that are always justified				
Sit-ins	26	28	13	30
Blockade of buildings	5	5	1	8
Assaulting police	4	2	—	6
Destroying draft board records	9	9	2	13
Shielding political prisoners	13	13	2	18
Using people as tools If purpose is morally justified	34	29	40	35
My Lai				
We are all responsible	40	41	40	39
No one is responsible	27	23	39	24

Table 62. Social and Personal Values Profile According to Political Affiliation

	Total	Demo-crat	Repub-lican	Other/None
	%	%	%	%
Values worth fighting a war for				
Counteracting aggression	50	47	61	46
Protecting our national interests	30	30	46	24
Containing the Communists	29	28	49	20
Maintaining our position of power in the world	19	21	28	12
Fighting for our honor	18	20	27	13
Keeping a commitment	14	14	21	10
Social restraints that are easily acceptable				
Prohibition against heroin	83	83	89	81
Power and authority of police	45	40	75	35
Prohibition against marijuana	42	39	68	33
Authority of a "boss" in work	36	34	53	29
Settling down to a routine	26	23	41	21
Keeping your views to yourself	16	16	23	12
Abiding by laws you don't agree with ..	13	13	23	9
Seen as morally wrong				
Taking things without paying for them	78	81	88	71
Destroying private property	72	73	80	68
Collecting welfare when you could work	75	74	84	70
Paying one's way through college by selling dope	63	63	80	54
Extramarital sex relations	57	57	73	49
Having children without marriage	42	44	60	31
Leaving the country to avoid the draft	28	24	48	21
Homosexuality	26	26	41	18
Casual sex relations	25	22	37	21
Very important personal values				
Love	87	87	87	86
Friendship	87	87	86	87
Education	74	79	75	70
Privacy	64	63	67	64
Family	65	68	73	59

(Continued on next page)

	Total	Demo-crat	Repub-lican	Other/None
	%	%	%	%
Doing things for others	59	61	61	57
Creativity	52	53	42	57
Being close to nature	47	44	44	51
Comfort	40	41	40	40
Living a clean moral life	34	33	44	29
Religion	31	32	45	23
Nationalism	27	25	53	17
Money	18	16	25	16
Beauty	19	13	23	22
Extent of belief in traditional values				
Business is entitled to a profit	85	87	93	79
Need for legally based authority	86	86	96	81
Children should respect parents	87	87	96	82
Importance of a meaningful career	79	80	88	73
Accept the legal consequences of breaking the law	70	70	82	64
Sacredness of private property	69	69	80	64
Competition encourages excellence ..	62	60	75	56
Saving to avoid dependency on others..	67	65	82	62
Hard work will always pay off	39	39	53	33
Welcome changes in values				
More emphasis on self-expression ...	80	82	68	84
Less emphasis on money	76	77	63	82
More acceptance of sexual freedom ..	56	56	36	64
More emphasis on law and order	50	48	71	41
More emphasis on technology	39	41	44	35
Less difference between the sexes ..	34	42	19	35
Marriage				
Agree that marriage is obsolete	34	33	23	40
Look forward to being legally married	61	65	74	52
Interested in having children	79	79	85	76
Living off the land has appeal (permanently/year or two)	43	41	28	51
Career choice				
Have no doubts about being able to make as much money as I want to ..	50	49	50	50
Have no doubts about being as successful as I want to	64	62	67	63

(Continued on next page)

	Total	Demo-crat	Repub-lican	Other/None
	%	%	%	%
Factors important in career choice				
Make a contribution	70	71	68	69
Challenge of the job	66	66	73	63
Self-expression	63	65	53	67
Job security	46	48	58	38
Chance to get ahead	35	35	42	31
Money	44	45	53	39
Prestige	22	24	31	17
Barriers to getting a desirable job				
Willingness to conform	24	21	12	32
Political views	15	16	6	19
Race	11	15	4	11
Self-identification				
Conservative/Moderate-Conservative ..	21	14	49	14
Middle of the Road	16	16	22	14
Liberal	53	64	29	55
Radical	10	6	—	17
Political party identification				
Democrat	36	100	—	—
Republican	21	—	100	—
Other/None	43	—	—	100
New Left identification				
New Left	11	12	1	15
Non-New Left	89	88	99	85
Psychology of affluence				
Career-Minded	61	63	72	54
Take-Affluence-for-Granted	39	37	28	46
Measure of alienation				
Personal values not shared by most Americans	32	30	21	40
Hard/intolerable to accept conventional life	33	33	13	43
Prefer to live in other country or society	30	31	21	35

CHAPTER 10
Male vs. Female

DESPITE THE GROWING EMPHASIS among young people on the blurring of the different roles of men and women, there are striking differences in the contrasting mood, attitudes, and values of the men and women students.

Women college students share with their male counterparts the same ambivalence about being happy in the present but confused about the future. Indeed, the tone and quality of the mood is, if anything, more pronounced among the women, who are even happier in their private lives and more confused about the future than the men students.

Yet underlying this seemingly similar general mood are discernible and meaningful differences in the outlook of the two groups.

More male students are skeptical, cynical, and pessimistic about the present state of our society and its institutions.

Women students are more adamant in their rejection of violence as a tactic or a philosophy and are readier to work within the Establishment—though not with business—to accomplish social change. They feel less strongly about the need for radical reform of many of our institutions, but they are also less optimistic about what lies ahead for the country, even in terms of the economy or ending the war in Vietnam.

The most striking differences between the men and women students are in the area of personal and traditional values and life style. Women students have a greater sense of commitment to doing things for others; set greater store on love, family, and living a clean moral life; are far more committed to marriage as a legal institution; and look forward with greater enthusiasm to being legally married and having children. More of the women students frown on the idea of

139

having extramarital relations, or of having children without being married. Even while they feel far more strongly than the men that women are oppressed, their career outlooks are very similar to the men students with the major emphasis being on the chance to make a contribution, the challenge of the job, and self-expression rather than on money or prestige. One out of two of the women, the same proportion as the men, has no doubts about being able to make as much money as she wants; two out of three, again the same proportion as the men, also have no doubts about being as successful as they want. Some of the most interesting similarities and differences between the men and women students include the following:

Demographic Differences

—Women students are younger. Sixty-three per cent of the female students are under 21 years of age compared to 50 per cent of the male students.
—Women students come from more affluent, better-educated backgrounds. Among women, 39 per cent have college educated fathers; 52 per cent have fathers who are professionals or hold executive and managerial positions. Among the men students, 31 per cent have college educated fathers; 46 per cent have fathers who are professionals or executives.
—Many women students plan on entering the scientific, engineering, and business worlds, but major in these fields far less than men. Among men, 43 per cent are majoring in science, engineering, or business, 38 per cent in humanities and social science, 9 per cent in education. For women, the figures are 28 per cent science, engineering and business, 38 per cent humanities, 26 per cent education.

Mood Profile

Women are:

—Happier than men (58% vs. 42%)
—More confused about the future (59% vs. 51%)
—Less skeptical (24% vs. 35%)
—Less agitated (9% vs. 16%)

140

Political Profile

On the whole, men and women college students share the same political views. The women, however, feel:

—More strongly that economic well-being in the country is unfairly distributed (85% vs. 79%).
—Less optimistic that the economy will improve this year (17% vs. 35%); less sanguine that the war will be over by the 1972 elections (9% vs. 16%).
—More convinced that women are oppressed (38% vs. 29%).
—Less concerned with the need for fundamental reform or doing away with the FBI or the trade unions.

Women students feel even more strongly than the men about working for social change within the Establishment rather than through protest organizations. Only 16 per cent of the women indicate a preference for working with protest movements compared to 22 per cent of the men. There are, however, decided differences in the groups within the Establishment with whom the men and women students prefer to work. Twenty-three per cent of the men pick the business leaders compared to only 14 per cent of the women. Fifty per cent of the women choose community leaders as their preference; only 33 per cent of the men make the same choice.

In terms of tactics, 62 per cent of the women are unqualifiedly opposed to violence, compared to 51 per cent of the men. Twenty-eight per cent of the women feel that using people as tools for the right purpose is morally justified in contrast to 39 per cent of the men with this view.

Social and Personal Values

It is in the context of moral and personal values and assessments, as we have noted earlier in this chapter, that there is the greatest divergence in views. Here the pattern is consistent:

On restraints: Women students find social restraints easier to accept then men with the exceptions of keeping one's views to oneself and

141

abiding by laws with which one doesn't agree. The ability to accept restraints more easily, however, is apparent in the case of:

—prohibition against heroin (87% vs. 79%);
—prohibition against marijuana (47% vs. 38%);
—power and authority of the police (49% vs. 41%);
—settling down to a routine (30% vs. 22%);
—the authority of a boss in work situations (40% vs. 32%).

On moral values: Women students take a far more moralistic stand than men. They see as morally wrong:

—taking things without paying for them (82% vs. 75%);
—destroying private property (77% vs. 68%);
—collecting welfare when you could work (78% vs. 72%);
—paying one's way through college by selling dope (69% vs. 57%);
—extramarital sex relations (67% vs. 48%);
—having children without marriage (49% vs. 35%);
—casual sex relations (33% vs. 16%).

Very Important Personal Values

To women, love is a more important personal value than to men (93% vs. 80%). So are:

—friendship (90% vs. 84%);
—education (78% vs. 70%);
—privacy (68% vs. 61%);
—family (73% vs. 58%);
—doing things for others (68% vs. 50%);
—religion (39% vs. 23%);
—living a clean moral life (40% vs. 28%).

They place less stress on money as an important personal value than men (13% vs. 22%), and also, interestingly enough, on beauty (15% vs. 23%).

Traditional vs. New Values

The acceptance of traditional values is on a par between men and women students in all instances except one. Women feel more strongly about saving to avoid dependency on others (73% vs. 62%).

On life-style values, the big debate between the two groups of students centers on marriage as an institution, and the entire question of more liberal sexual relations. Not only do more women question the morality of premarital sexual relations, but they are more divided than men on the very concept of greater sexual freedom. While a high figure of one out of two women (48%) would welcome more acceptance of sexual freedom, their numbers are dwarfed by the 64 per cent of the men who are eager for this change.

The reverse trend is apparent in views on marriage and children. Seventy-two per cent of the women look forward to being legally married compared to 51 per cent of the men; 83 per cent look forward to having children, compared to 75 per cent of the men.

Finally, there is the question of career aspirations. As indicated, approximately equal numbers of men and women indicate no doubts about being able to make as much money as is wanted (48% vs. 51%), nor about being as successful as is wanted (63% vs. 64%).

Women students, however, place even more stress on career choice than men as to:

—making a contribution (73% vs. 66%);
—the challenge of the job (70% vs. 63%).

And less emphasis on:

—prestige (16% vs. 28%);
—money (39% vs. 49%);
—and especially the chance to get ahead (26% vs. 43%), with this last difference reflecting either their feelings about the present unequal position of women, or their hopes for marriage and children —or both.

See Tables 63–66 for details.

143

Table **63.**   Demographic Profile According to Sex

	Total	Male	Female
	%	%	%
Sex			
Male	51	100	—
Female	49	—	100
Age			
Under 21 years	56	50	63
21 years and older	44	50	37
Father's education			
High school or less	44	47	41
Some college	21	22	20
College graduate/post-graduate	35	31	39
Father's occupation			
Professional/managerial	49	46	52
White collar	18	20	17
Blue collar	19	20	17
Other	14	14	14
Race			
White	87	86	87
Non-white	13	14	13
Major			
Humanities/social science	38	38	38
Education	18	9	26
Science/engineering/business	35	43	28
Undecided/other	9	10	8
Religion			
Protestant	39	36	42
Catholic	21	19	23
Jewish	9	11	7
Other/none	31	34	28
Employment			
Working part time/full time	49	50	48
Not working	51	50	52
Region			
Northeast	24	25	23
North Central	27	26	28
South	24	23	25
West	25	26	24

Table **64.**   Mood Profile According to Sex

	Total %	Male %	Female %
Change of mood since last year			
More involved in private life	61	64	58
Happier in personal life	55	51	60
More serious about studying	48	50	46
More fearful of future job chances	50	45	54
More doubtful of chance to change society	30	31	29
More determined to do something	27	27	27
More feeling of individual powerlessness	29	30	28
More doubtful of political leaders' honesty	52	54	51
Less accepting of violence	44	42	46
Less alienated	33	30	37
Less politically conservative	41	42	41
Less sure of country's health	42	41	42
Current mood			
Confused about the future	55	51	59
Happy	50	42	58
Skeptical	30	35	24
Involved	28	26	29
Frustrated	27	27	28
Satisfied	24	20	27
Discouraged	21	20	22
Cynical	15	17	12
Agitated	13	16	9

Table **65.**   Political Profile According to Sex

	Total %	Male %	Female %
Country is faring pretty badly/very badly	62	62	62
Believe the war will be over by 1972 election	13	16	9
Believe the economy will improve this year	26	35	17
Agree that country is a "sick society"	45	47	44

(Continued on next page)

	Total	Male	Female
	%	%	%

Believe that radical change is needed/system ought to be replaced 27 27 26

Real power in the country vested in giant corporations/financial institutions 58 59 56

System not democratic—the special interests propagandize the mass of people 57 57 58

Agree strongly or partially that:

	Total	Male	Female
Business too concerned with profits . . . not enough with public responsibility	93	92	93
Economic well-being unjustly and unfairly distributed	81	79	85
We are a racist nation	80	81	81
Our two-party system offers no real alternative	73	74	73
People's privacy is being destroyed	83	84	81
Police should not hesitate to use force	53	55	53
Minority must not impose its will on the majority	52	54	51
Too much concern for welfare bum, not enough for person struggling to make a living	68	68	69
Radicals of the Left are as much a threat as radicals of the Right	87	85	89

Groups that cannot be assured a fair trial

	Total	Male	Female
Black Panthers	65	64	66
Radicals	49	49	49
Drug addicts	46	45	48
Middle-class blacks	29	29	28
Indians	40	40	39
Manufacturers of defective products	18	22	15
Polluters	25	27	24

Groups that are oppressed

	Total	Male	Female
Blacks	81	81	81
Women	33	29	38
College students	27	30	25
Homosexuals	84	81	86

Needs fundamental reform or should be done away with

	Total	Male	Female
Big business	46	45	45
The military	67	69	67

(Continued on next page)

146

	Total	Male	Female
	%	%	%
The trade unions	39	45	33
The political parties	54	54	54
The FBI	39	43	35
The Supreme Court	24	21	26
The Constitution	18	19	17
Best method for creating social change			
Individual working in his own community	78	73	83
Changing the outlook of the public	55	55	56
Create respect for law and order	41	39	43
Organize new political party	25	27	23
Nationalize private industry	15	15	15
Create conditions for revolution	11	13	9
Prefer to work with protest movement rather than with the Establishment	19	22	16
Within Establishment prefer to work with:			
Community leaders	41	33	50
Business leaders	18	23	14
Federal agencies	15	13	17
Candidates for political office	12	13	11
Unqualifiedly opposed to violence	56	51	62
Tactics that are always justified			
Sit-ins	26	27	24
Blockade of buildings	5	6	4
Assaulting police	4	5	2
Destroying draft board records	9	10	8
Shielding political prisoners	13	15	11
Using people as tools if purpose is morally justified	34	39	28
My Lai			
We are all responsible	40	35	45
No one is responsible	27	26	27

147

Table 66.   Social and Personal Values Profile According to Sex

	Total %	Male %	Female %
Values worth fighting a war for			
Counteracting aggression	50	50	49
Protecting our national interests	30	31	29
Containing the Communists	29	25	33
Maintaining our position of power in the world	19	17	20
Fighting for our honor	18	18	19
Keeping a commitment	14	12	16
Social restraints that are easily acceptable			
Prohibition against heroin	83	79	87
Power and authority of police	45	41	49
Prohibition against marijuana	42	38	47
Authority of a "boss" in work	36	32	40
Settling down to a routine	26	22	30
Keeping your views to yourself	16	15	16
Abiding by laws you don't agree with	13	13	14
Seen as morally wrong			
Taking things without paying for them	78	75	82
Destroying private property	72	68	77
Collecting welfare when you could work	75	72	78
Paying one's way through college by selling dope	63	57	69
Extramarital sex relations	57	48	67
Having children without marriage	42	35	49
Leaving the country to avoid the draft	28	28	29
Homosexuality	26	24	27
Casual sex relations	25	16	33
Very important personal values			
Love	87	80	93
Friendship	87	84	90
Education	74	70	78
Privacy	64	61	68
Family	65	58	73
Doing things for others	59	50	68
Creativity	52	51	54
Being close to nature	47	44	50
Comfort	40	40	41

(Continued on next page)

	Total	Male	Female
	%	%	%
Living a clean moral life	34	28	40
Religion	31	23	39
Nationalism	27	26	28
Money	18	22	13
Beauty	19	23	15
Extent of belief in traditional values			
Business is entitled to a profit	85	82	87
Need for legally based authority	86	84	88
Children should respect parents	87	86	88
Importance of a meaningful career	79	78	80
Accept the legal consequences of breaking the law	70	70	69
Sacredness of private property	69	66	72
Competition encourages excellence	62	67	57
Saving to avoid dependency on others	67	62	73
Hard work will always pay off	39	42	37
Welcome changes in values			
More emphasis on self-expression	80	79	81
Less emphasis on money	76	71	81
More acceptance of sexual freedom	56	64	48
More emphasis on law and order	50	48	52
More emphasis on technology	39	43	34
Less difference between the sexes	34	35	34
Marriage			
Agree that marriage is obsolete	34	37	30
Look forward to being legally married	61	51	72
Interested in having children	79	75	83
Living off the land has appeal (permanently/ year or two)	43	45	41
Career choice			
Have no doubts about being able to make as much money as I want to	50	51	48
Have no doubts about being as successful as I want to	64	64	63
Factors important in career choice			
Make a contribution	70	66	73
Challenge of the job	66	63	70
Self-expression	63	63	63

(Continued on next page)

	Total	Male	Female
	%	%	%
Job security	46	48	43
Chance to get ahead	35	43	26
Money	44	49	39
Prestige	22	28	16
Barriers to getting a desirable job			
Willingness to conform	24	30	17
Political views	15	20	10
Race	11	12	10
Self-identification			
Conservative/Moderate-Conservative	21	22	21
Middle of the Road	16	14	19
Liberal	53	50	55
Radical	10	14	5
Political party identification			
Democrat	36	35	37
Republican	21	21	21
Other/None	43	44	42
New Left identification			
New Left	11	15	7
Non-New Left	89	85	93
Psychology of affluence			
Career-Minded	61	59	62
Take-Affluence-for-Granted	39	41	38
Measure of alienation			
Personal values not shared by most Americans	32	37	28
Hard/Intolerable to accept conventional life	33	46	34
Prefer to live in other country or society	30	32	29

CHAPTER 11

Values and Attitudes of Minority-Group Students

THIRTEEN PER CENT of our sample of college students were non-white. Of this group about nine out of ten (11% of the 13%) were black. Thus we have taken the liberty of referring to the non-white students in this chapter as "blacks" with the understanding that it does contain a sprinkling of Puerto Rican, Mexican-American, and oriental students.

From many points of view, the black student is the most conflicted young person on the American campus. As a member of the black "elite," the black student recognizes the opportunities that will be open and available with a college diploma—but on the other hand there is also a deep sense of commitment to uneducated and discriminated-against black people and a loyalty to the young militants.

Thus it becomes exceedingly difficult to find the precise words which fully convey the complexity of the black student's outlook, values and mood.

There is frustration and determination. Thirty-eight per cent of the black students say they have a greater feeling of individual powerlessness now than the year before; but 43 per cent are more determined to do something now. (This compares with only 25 per cent of the white students who feel this way.)

Two out of three black students (68%) have no doubts about being personally as successful as they want, but 38 per cent—10 percentage points more than white students—are even more doubtful of having a chance to change society than the year before.

There is anger at many of the country's institutions, including the Constitution and the political parties; there is anger at how the country is going and at the inequities of the social system; there is despair over social injustice, particularly against the blacks; there is determination to change things, but without violence unless all else fails.

Eighty per cent of the black students are opposed to violence except as a last resort. Militancy, yes; violence, perferably no.

Militancy has brought a minority of the blacks to radicalism (19%); many of them are adopting the values of the counterculture. Forty-six per cent say they find it hard or intolerable to accept a conventional life styles. Yet large numbers are also seeking for themselves some of the very values which the Post-Affluents scorn—money, status, comfort.

The conflicts, the loneliness of the black student are indicated in the descriptive and tabular results which follow.

Demographic Differences

The black student is younger and, as could be anticipated, is from a less affluent, less well-educated background than fellow white students. Sixty-one per cent of the black students are under 21; 66 per cent come from homes in which the father had at best a high school education.

Despite the publicity about the opportunities awaiting black students in the business world, a larger proportion (64%) than among white students (55%) are studying humanities or education.

In terms of geography, it is interesting to note that black students are coming to the campus in almost equal numbers from all regions of the country.

Mood Profile

The mood of the black student is tense, serious, and frustrated—not about his or her own chance to succeed—but about conditions in the country and the fate and treatment of black people.

Compared to the year before, as well as compared to other fellow students, the black student is less happy, more serious about studying, more determined to do something, but more doubtful of a chance to change society. On only one score is the black student in a more optimistic frame of mind compared to white students. Fewer black than white students are fearful about future job opportunities.

152

Political Profile

Black students far more than white believe that the country is faring badly, that we are a sick society, and that radical change is needed. Seventy-five per cent of the black students believe that the system is not democratic compared to 55 per cent of white students.

Only 12 per cent of the black students feel that the economy will improve this year compared to 29 per cent of the white students.

Black students also agree even more emphatically (90%), that economic well-being is unjustly and unfairly distributed. Nine out of ten say we are a racist society.

Considerably fewer black students, however, agree with the majority of white students in believing that the police should not hesitate to use force, that the minority must not impose its will on the majority, or that too much concern is being shown for the welfare "bum."

Social Justice

A majority of black students believe that the following groups cannot be assured a fair trial: Black Panthers (80%); radicals (63%); drug addicts (60%); Indians (57%).

They are divided on the ability of middle-class blacks to get a fair trial; 49 per cent feel they cannot. In every instance mentioned, however, they are far more dubious than white students on the quality of social justice available in the United States.

Then, too, far more than whites, they see blacks (89%), women (44%), and college students (35%) as members of oppressed groups.

Institutions

Compared to white students, blacks on the campus single out the Constitution as an institution that needs fundamental reform or should be done away with. Forty per cent of the blacks feel this way compared to 14 per cent of the white students.

Blacks are also more critical than whites of the political parties (63% vs. 52%) and the FBI (46% vs. 38%).

153

Creating Social Change

More blacks than whites see the need for organizing a new political party (34% vs. 24%) or for creating conditions for revolution (23% vs. 9%) or nationalizing private industry (20% vs. 14%) as the best method for creating social change. The majority, however (68%), join with whites in feeling that the most effective means of achieving social change is through individuals working in communities and/or changing the outlook of the public (55%).

Militancy

The militancy of the black students is expressed in a greater preference for working with the protest movement to effect change than is found among white students. Thirty-one per cent of the black students prefer working with the protest movement compared to 17 per cent of the white students. Black students also believe to a greater extent than white students that it is justifiable to use people as tools if the purpose is morally right (45% vs. 32%).

Social Values

On War as a Value: The large majority of black students reject the justifications of war, whether the purpose is counteracting aggression, protecting our national interest, containing the Communists, maintaining our position of power, or keeping a commitment.

Social Restraints That Are Easily Acceptable: Black students find it harder than white students to accept the prohibition against heroin (74% vs. 85%); the power and authority of the police (25% vs. 48%); the prohibition against marijuana (39% vs. 43%); and the authority of a "boss" in a work situation (29% vs. 37%).

Seen as Morally Wrong: Fewer black students than white tend to consider the following as morally wrong:

—Taking things without paying for them (67% vs. 80%)
—Destroying private property (63% vs. 74%)

—Collecting welfare when you can work (68% vs. 76%)
—Paying one's way through college by selling dope (54% vs. 64%)

They share to almost the same extent as white students ideas about marriage and sex:

—Extramarital sex relations (53% vs. 58%)
—Having children without marriage (37% vs. 43%)
—Casual sex relations (18% vs. 26%)

Personal Values

Coming in the main from deprived rather than affluent homes, more black students place value on money (29% vs. 16%) and comfort (57% vs. 38%) than white students. More black students also place emphasis on education (80% vs. 73%); family (74% vs. 64%); and privacy (72% vs. 63%).

Compared to white students, they place less emphasis on friendship (74% vs. 89%) and nationalism (16% vs. 29%).

Traditional Values

Black students share most of the views of white students on traditional values but are more convinced that:

—Competition encourages excellence (73% vs. 60%)
—Hard work will always pay off (53% vs. 37%)
—Saving avoids dependency on others (77% vs. 66%)

Marriage

Black students accept more than white students the idea that marriage is obsolete (49% vs. 31%)—but look forward in about equal numbers to being legally married (60% vs. 61%) and to having children (78% vs. 79%).

After the bitter struggle to get ahead, far fewer of the black students are looking forward to living off the land (28% vs. 45%).

Careers

Forty-five per cent of the blacks have no doubts about being able to make as much money as is wanted compared to 50 per cent for white students. Sixty-eight per cent have no doubts about being as successful as is wanted (63% for white).

In choosing a career, black students place more weight than whites on money, chance to get ahead and job security.

Statistical findings covering the views and attitudes of black and white students are covered in Tables 67 through 70, which follow.

Table 67.   Demographic Profile According to Race

	Total	White	Non-white
	%	%	%
Sex			
Male	51	50	54
Female	49	50	46
Age			
Under 21 years	56	55	61
21 years and older	44	45	39
Father's education			
High school or less	44	40	66
Some college	21	22	16
College graduate/post-graduate	35	38	18
Father's occupation			
Professional/managerial	49	53	26
White collar	18	19	13
Blue collar	19	17	29
Other	14	11	32
Race			
White	87	100	—
Non-white	13	—	100

(Continued on next page)

	Total	White	Non-white
	%	%	%
Major			
Humanities/social science	38	38	41
Education	18	17	23
Science/engineering/business	35	35	32
Undecided/other	9	10	4
Religion			
Protestant	39	38	43
Catholic	21	22	17
Jewish	9	11	1
Other/none	31	29	39
Employment			
Working part time/full time	49	50	45
Not working	51	50	55
Region			
Northeast	24	25	20
North Central	27	27	25
South	24	24	28
West	25	24	27

Table 68.   Mood Profile According to Race

	Total	White	Non-white
	%	%	%
Change of mood since last year			
More involved in private life	61	60	64
Happier in personal life	55	57	46
More serious about studying	48	47	52
More fearful of future job chances	50	51	40
More doubtful of chance to change society	30	28	38
More determined to do something	27	25	43
More feeling of individual powerlessness	29	28	38
More doubtful of political leaders' honesty	52	52	56

(Continued on next page)

157

	Total	White	Non-white
	%	%	%
Less accepting of violence	44	45	38
Less alienated	33	33	32
Less politically conservative	41	42	41
Less sure of country's health	42	42	42
Current mood			
Confused about the future	55	55	54
Happy	50	51	41
Skeptical	30	29	34
Involved	28	26	38
Frustrated	27	27	32
Satisfied	24	25	16
Discouraged	21	21	23
Cynical	15	14	15
Agitated	13	12	20

Table 69.   Political Profile According to Race

	Total	White	Non-white
	%	%	%
Country is faring pretty badly/very badly	62	60	77
Believe the war will be over by 1972 election ...	13	13	11
Believe the economy will improve this year	26	29	12
Agree that country is a "sick society"	45	42	67
Believe that radical change is needed/system ought to be replaced	27	23	50
Real power in the country vested in giant corporations/financial institutions	58	57	60
System not democratic—the special interests propagandize the mass of people	57	55	75
Agree strongly or partially that: Business too concerned with profits . . . not enough with public responsibility	93	92	96

(*Continued on next page*)

	Total	White	Non-white
	%	%	%
Economic well-being unjustly and unfairly distributed	81	81	90
We are a racist nation	80	79	90
Our two-party system offers no real alternative	73	73	76
People's privacy is being destroyed	83	82	89
Police should not hesitate to use force	53	55	44
Minority must not impose its will on the majority	52	55	34
Too much concern for welfare bum, not enough for person struggling to make a living	68	71	56
Radicals of the Left are as much a threat as radicals of the Right	87	88	82
Groups that cannot be assured a fair trial			
Black Panthers	65	63	80
Radicals	49	47	63
Drug addicts	46	44	60
Middle-class blacks	29	26	49
Indians	40	37	57
Manufacturers of defective products	18	18	20
Polluters	25	26	25
Groups that are oppressed			
Blacks	81	80	89
Women	33	32	44
College students	27	26	35
Homosexuals	84	84	84
Needs fundamental reform or should be done away with			
Big business	46	45	47
The military	67	68	67
The trade unions	39	39	35
The political parties	54	52	63
The FBI	39	38	46
The Supreme Court	24	23	29
The Constitution	18	14	40
Best method for creating social change			
Individual working in his own community	78	79	68
Changing the outlook of the public	55	56	55
Create respect for law and order	41	42	31
Organize new political party	25	24	34

(Continued on next page)

159

	Total %	White %	Non-white %
Nationalize private industry	15	14	20
Create conditions for revolution	11	9	23
Prefer to work with protest movement rather than with the Establishment	19	17	31
Within Establishment prefer to work with:			
Community leaders	41	41	44
Business leaders	18	19	13
Federal agencies	15	14	19
Candidates for political office	12	13	7
Unqualifiedly opposed to violence	56	60	28
Tactics that are always justified			
Sit-ins	26	25	28
Blockade of buildings	5	5	10
Assaulting police	4	3	7
Destroying draft board records	9	8	13
Shielding political prisoners	13	12	17
Using people as tools if purpose is morally justified	34	32	45
My Lai			
We are all responsible	40	41	32
No one is responsible	27	27	28

Table **70.**   Social and Personal Values Profile According to Race

	Total %	White %	Non-white %
Values worth fighting a war for			
Counteracting aggression	50	51	43
Protecting our national interests	30	30	34
Containing the Communists	29	30	26
Maintaining our position of power in the world	19	18	27
Fighting for our honor	18	18	24
Keeping a commitment	14	14	15

(Continued on next page)

	Total	White	Non-white
	%	%	%
Social restraints that are easily acceptable			
Prohibition against heroin	83	85	74
Power and authority of police	45	48	25
Prohibition against marijuana	42	43	39
Authority of a "boss" in work	36	37	29
Settling down to a routine	26	26	23
Keeping your views to yourself	16	16	14
Abiding by laws you don't agree with	13	14	8
Seen as morally wrong			
Taking things without paying for them	78	80	67
Destroying private property	72	74	63
Collecting welfare when you could work	75	76	68
Paying one's way through college by selling dope	63	64	54
Extramarital sex relations	57	58	53
Having children without marriage	42	43	37
Leaving the country to avoid the draft	28	28	27
Homosexuality	26	26	23
Casual sex relations	25	26	18
Very important personal values			
Love	87	87	83
Friendship	87	89	74
Education	74	73	80
Privacy	64	63	72
Family	65	64	74
Doing things for others	59	60	54
Creativity	52	52	53
Being close to nature	47	48	40
Comfort	40	38	57
Living a clean moral life	34	33	37
Religion	31	30	34
Nationalism	27	29	16
Money	18	16	29
Beauty	19	20	14
Extent of belief in traditional values			
Business is entitled to a profit	85	85	81
Need for legally based authority	86	87	80

(Continued on next page)

161

	Total	White	Non-white
	%	%	%
Children should respect parents	87	86	92
Importance of a meaningful career	79	79	80
Accept the legal consequences of breaking the law	70	71	60
Sacredness of private property	69	70	65
Competition encourages excellence	62	60	73
Saving to avoid dependency on others	67	66	77
Hard work will always pay off	39	37	53
Welcome changes in values			
More emphasis on self-expression	80	80	80
Less emphasis on money	76	76	75
More acceptance of sexual freedom	56	55	60
More emphasis on law and order	50	51	40
More emphasis on technology	39	39	41
Less difference between the sexes	34	33	38
Marriage			
Agree that marriage is obsolete	34	31	49
Look forward to being legally married	61	61	60
Interested in having children	79	79	78
Living off the land has appeal (permanently/ year or two)	43	45	28
Career choice			
Have no doubts about being able to make as much money as I want to	50	50	45
Have no doubts about being as successful as I want to	64	63	68
Factors important in career choice			
Make a contribution	70	71	63
Challenge of the job	66	67	60
Self-expression	63	63	65
Job security	46	45	53
Chance to get ahead	35	32	51
Money	44	43	53
Prestige	22	22	23

(Continued on next page)

VALUES AND ATTITUDES OF MINORITY-GROUP STUDENTS

	Total %	White %	Non-white %
Barriers to getting a desirable job			
Willingness to conform	24	24	24
Political views	15	13	27
Race	11	2	66
Self-identification			
Conservative/Moderate-Conservative	21	22	18
Middle of the Road	16	16	15
Liberal	53	54	48
Radical	10	8	19
Political party identification			
Democrat	36	34	49
Republican	21	23	7
Other/None	43	43	44
New Left identification			
New Left	11	10	13
Non-New Left	89	90	87
Psychology of affluence			
Career-Minded	61	61	60
Take-Affluence-for-Granted	39	39	40
Measure of alienation			
Personal values not shared by most Americans	32	32	37
Hard/Intolerable to accept conventional life ..	33	31	46
Prefer to live in other country or society	30	30	35

163

PART III
The New Naturalism
by Daniel Yankelovich

[I]

"GREAT IDEAS often enter reality in strange guises and with disgusting alliances."[1] This phrase, from Whitehead's *Adventures of Ideas*, raises an intriguing question about the college youth movement. Whitehead was referring to the emergence in Western civilization of the idea of the essential equality of men, and to the vicissitudes of this idea over three millennia as our civilization moved from the presumption of slavery to the presumption of equality. Might the college student movement conceivably harbor an idea of comparable importance? Should its claim to transform our moral sensibilities and national life styles be taken seriously? Are we witnessing the growth of an authentic and, in the European sense of the word, *serious* movement in American history, or merely a nervous spasm elicited in response to the nervous-making events of our time?

In the course of our research with college students over the past seven years, I have gradually come to regard these questions as the most crucial ones that can be raised about the student movement. Critics of student protest have often let their prejudices and emotions interfere with their judgment. Those who are offended by the long hair, the rioting, the open sexuality, and the challenge to authority see only strange guises and disgusting alliances. Devotees of the counterculture, on the other hand, romanticize the movement and greet each strange new guise it assumes as the inspired expression of a great idea. But is it not possible that such judgments—on both sides—are half-truths which, even though they seem to contradict each other, actually

---

[1] Alfred North Whitehead, *Adventures of Ideas*. Macmillan, 1956.

167

form a single truth? Is it not likely, as Whitehead implies, that an important new idea struggling to gain clarity of expression will assume various transitional forms, some of them disturbing or even ugly and others contaminated by the circumstances of the moment? Indeed, do not *all* great ideas that find expression in mass movements first enter history in strange, transitional guises?

Our own view, arrived at after years of deliberation, is that Whitehead's formula correctly sums up the student movement: the movement *does* harbor a great idea and that idea has entered current American reality in many strange and misleading guises.

Unfortunately, years will pass before we shall be able to grasp the nature and full significance of the idea. Important historical movements do not yield up their secrets that easily, especially to those caught up in the midst of them. Yet, premature though it may be, we can begin to clarify the essence of the idea and divest it of its purely incidental and circumstantial features. In so doing, we should, however, acknowledge that we move beyond the professional neutrality of social science and encroach on the domain of social philosophy where one's own views and values are forced out into the open. This point is emphasized in order to distinguish this personal and interpretive part of the book from its scientific sections.

[II]

No idea is ever wholly new, least of all an idea embraced by a mass movement. Originality and mass support rarely go together. For an idea to be embraced by large numbers of people it must be "in the air" for a long period of time even though it may later burst forth in a seeming explosion of spontaneity. Truly original ideas are first formulated by thinkers who live and work in advance of their time and who sense some hidden tendency of the age. Years, decades, even generations later when its impact has become more evident, the idea is rediscovered. It then emerges in a wide variety of forms and is formulated by many observers simultaneously. If the idea happens to respond to people's unsatisfied moral urges or if it holds out the promise of meeting some inherent human need frustrated by the society, it then begins to inspire a mass following.

The idea energizing the student movement does both: it offers a banner around which young people, hungry for a new moral faith, can rally; and it promises to fulfill inherent human needs which are now being frustrated. Conceptually, the idea is neither wholly original nor yet a platitude. It has, in fact, been a recurring theme of our civilization for hundreds of years, though it has probably not been urged in so compelling and novel a form since the time of Rousseau.

The essence of the idea is that we must initiate a new stage in man's relatedness to nature and the natural. In the hierarchy of values that constitute man's conception of the *summum bonum*, the student-led cultural revolution elevates nature and the natural to the highest position. Whatever is "natural" is deemed to be good; whatever is artificial and opposed to the natural is bad. But what is natural and what is opposed to nature? The answer is by no means self-evident. Indeed, the power of the underlying idea lies in its specificity rather than in its general form. We have identified eighteen meanings of the natural embraced by the student movement. All of them are interrelated so that they form a single unity. Some of the meanings are obvious, others are subtle. Some are superficial expressions of life-styles which students try on and then abandon like so many one-night stands. Other meanings are fundamental to man's existence. Some meanings are intimate and personal, others are broadly political. Some will endure, others will fade from the scene. Compositely, these meanings add up to a new world view, a philosophy of life and of nature capable of transforming man's relationship to himself and his society.

Here are some of the varied aspects of "nature" and the "natural" which reside either implicitly or explicitly in the student movement's philosophy of nature:

1. Moving the Darwinian concept of nature as "survival of the fittest" into the background; placing emphasis instead on the interdependence of all things and species in nature.

2. Placing emphasis on sensory experience rather than on conceptual knowledge.

3. Living physically close to nature, in the open, off the land.

4. Living in groups rather than as isolated individuals or in "artificial" social units such as the nuclear family.

5. Rejecting hypocrisy, "white lies," and other social artifices.

6. Deemphasizing realms of knowledge illuminated by science; instead, celebrating the unknown, the mystical, and the mysterious elements of nature.

7. Emphasizing cooperation rather than competition.

8. Embracing the existentialist emphasis on being rather than doing or planning.

9. Deemphasizing detachment, objectivity, and noninvolvement as methods for finding truth; arriving at truth by direct experience, participation, and involvement.

10. Looking and feeling natural, hence rejecting makeup, bras, suits, ties, artificially groomed hairstyles.

11. Expressing one's experience nonverbally; avoiding the literary and the stylized as artificial and unnatural; relying instead on exclamations, silence, vibrations, and various nonverbal forms of expression to communicate and respond.

12. Rejecting "official" and hence artificial forms of authority; authority is to be gained by winning respect and is not a matter of automatic entitlement by virtue of position or official title.

13. Rejecting mastery over nature, emphasizing harmony with nature.

14. Deemphasizing organization, rationalization, cost-effectiveness.

15. Emphasizing self-knowledge, introspection, discovery of one's natural self.

16. Emphasizing the community rather than the individual.

17. Rejecting mores and rules that interfere with natural expression and function (e.g., conventional sexual morality).

18. Emphasizing the preservation of the natural environment at the expense of economic growth and technology.

These varying conceptions of nature and the natural grow out of, and are a reaction against, the dominant modes of thinking in American culture as represented by technology, rationalism, and traditional middle-class sensibility. Here is a random concatenation of words and phrases that capture as well as any formal definition the sensibility which the student's cultural revolution rejects:

Professional . . . system . . . planning for the future . . . conceptual framework . . . experiment . . . organization . . . detachment . . . management . . . verification . . . facts . . . technology . . . cost-effectiveness . . . theory . . . rationalization . . . efficiency . . . measurement . . . statistical controls . . . manipulate . . . mechanization . . . institutions . . . power . . . determinism . . . intelligence testing . . . abstract thought . . . programming . . . calculate . . . objectify . . . behaviorism . . . modification of the human environment . . . liberal . . . molded to specification . . . genetic planning . . . achievement.

The counterculture is well named: it defines itself, at least in part, in terms of what it opposes. And what it opposes constitutes a huge part of our culture. Yet, as the varied definitions of nature and the natural listed above suggest, the positive side of the counterculture, though often submerged beneath its oppositional tendencies, is the more significant one. We would like to call special attention to three themes in the new naturalism of the student movement—the stress on community rather than on the individual, the apparent anti-intellectualism and emphasis on the nonrational, and the search for sacredness in nature.

The Community vs. the Individual

It is a mistake to think of student values in conventional political terms. The student movement is generally identified with the Left and with political radicalism. And, to be sure, many of its notions and alliances are liberal or radical. But some of its leading ideas, especially those relating to community, have deep roots in conservative tradition. If we were to trace liberal and conservative ideologies his-

171

torically, we could differentiate them by referring to their opposing positions on such fundamental matters as equality, authority, and community. By these criteria, the student's cultural revolution can be characterized as liberal or radical on equality and authority, and conservative on community. In the past, authority and community have been linked together, almost always on the conservative side, while a concern with equality has generally been associated with political liberalism. It is such novel combinations and juxtapositions of ideas that make the student movement provocative: at least some of the old stereotypes are being rethought along fresh lines.

Community is an idea of pivotal importance in nineteenth-century thought, especially, as Nisbet points out, conservative thought.[2] Historically, the symbolism and human bonds conveyed by the idea of community formed the conservative image of the good society in contrast to the kind of society dominated by individualism.

Nisbet describes the notion of community in 19th and 20th century thought as follows: "[Community] encompasses all forms of relationships which are characterized by a high degree of personal intimacy, emotional depth, moral commitment, social cohesion, and continuity in time. Community is founded on man conceived in his wholeness rather than in one or another of the roles, taken separately, that he may hold in a social order. It draws its psychological strength from levels of motivation deeper than those of mere volition or interest, and it achieves its fulfillment in a submergence of individual will that is not possible in unions of mere convenience or rational assent. Community is a fusion of feeling and thought, of tradition and commitment, of membership and volition. It may be found in, or be given symbolic expression by, locality, religion, nation, race, occupation or crusade . . . Fundamental to the strength of the bond of community is the real or imagined antithesis formed in the same social setting by the noncommunal relations of competition or conflict, utility or contractual assent. These, by their relative impersonality and anonymity, highlight the close personal ties of community."[3]

The task of restoring, preserving, and creating new forms of com-

---

[2] Robert A. Nisbet, *The Sociological Tradition*. Basic Books, 1966.
[3] *Ibid.,* pp. 47–48.

munity has, in fact, haunted the Western mind ever since the Middle Ages. It is as if the great victories in succeeding centuries won by Protestantism, individualism, rationalism, science, and industrialization all were gained at a terrible cost—the sacrifice of community. The cost was minimized in the headiness of newly won freedom, democracy, and material progress. Yet, as our history unfolds, the élan of our technological/materialist society wears down. A terrible loneliness and sense of isolation breaks through at the society's greatest points of vulnerability. In our present type of society, many of the human bonds of community—bonds seen as so necessary to the spirit as to be constitutive of all that is humanly natural—have come apart. Ordinary human decency, repose, and stability depend on restoring them.

Some such notion of community—its roots in human nature, its pivotal importance, its opposition to individualism, and its terrible absence in our society—lies at the very heart of the student conception of nature and the natural. Hume was the first of the modern philosophers to stress as inherent and "natural" human characteristics the qualities of goodness, giving, and cooperation—qualities implied by the student use of community. In our day, society is seen by the student movement as suppressing these qualities as ruthlessly as the cramping moral codes of the Victorian era suppressed sexuality.

The Nonrational

Perhaps no other aspect of the cultural revolution is as poorly understood—and as widely misinterpreted—as student mistrust of rational, conceptual, calculative, and abstract modes of thought. Faculty scholars, in particular, are appalled at the seeming anti-intellectualism of the counterculture with its stress on sense experience and what often seems to be an ideological commitment to inarticulateness.

The scholarly professor of English Literature begins to wonder about his own sanity after a long day's experience with the glories of the English language being reduced to a repetitive series of "like," "you know," "freaked out," etc. The historian questions his own commitment to the past after spending months with students for whom only the present and the future seem to exist. Time itself loses its ordered sequence, becoming a patternless series of quantum leaps from one sensory immersion to another.

The student movement reserves its most brutal shock, however, for those logically minded managers, technologists, engineers, professors of business administration, planners, accountants, experimenters, and quantifiers for whom rational, orderly, and logical methods are the royal road to truth. For these professionals—and they are the men who keep our society running—student disdain for rational procedures is incomprehensible. In such attitudes, should they be generalized, they see the destruction of all they have built. And they are probably correct. Even within the counterculture itself, the disdain for technique takes its toll. Commune-baked bread is often hard, flat and tasteless; the commune-manufactured belts fall apart (how many belts, after all, do we need?); and commune-based law firms who reject disciplined thought win few cases.

As our society is presently constituted, service to one's fellowman, offered with compassion but without knowledge, can be a menace to both giver and recipient. Carried to its extreme, rejection of concepts, technique, professionalism, know-how, and methods of rationalization can be sloppy and self-defeating. Unless the cultural revolution is to be confined to enclaves of elitist dropouts with well-heeled parents, it must learn to coexist with the technological thrust of our society.

If the new naturalism as an idea system is to have a constructive impact on the society, it must presuppose the existence of an affluent economy with a technological base. Charles Reich to the contrary, Consciousness III cannot thrive unless Consciousness II also thrives. The relationship between them is symbiotic, not mutually exclusive.

With these qualifications registered, we come to our main point which is that the student critique of the rational, the technical and the abstract is not mainly negative; indeed, it is not a *vote against* but a *quest for* other modes of understanding. Some of the greatest philosophers of our century, notably Wittgenstein, Heidegger, Whitehead, and others, have performed their own critique of so-called rational thought and have arrived at conclusions not that different from those embraced by the counterculture. Coming from widely divergent traditions of philosophy, these seminal thinkers concur on one central conclusion; namely, that our equation of abstract logical thinking with

174

knowing, with truth, and with rationality itself is based on a profound misunderstanding created by fallacies built into the epistemological assumptions of the past three hundred years of Western philosophy and science.

The marriage of abstract thought with quantitative methods—what might be called "McNamaraism" even though McNamara himself has now transcended his own methodology—creates a remarkably restricted mentality. When applied to certain narrow problems of logistics or of conditioning pigeons in the laboratory it can be excellent. But it fails utterly when social/political reality is to be grasped, Vietnam being an example. An argument can be made that rigid adherence to McNamaraism, far from being the essence of rationality, is itself a virulent form of irrationalism. There is something irrational about the evangelical dogmatism of the B. F. Skinners and the other Dr. Strangeloves of our era who, skimming the surface of reality and imposing upon it the most doctrinaire of *a priori* premises, insist upon their approach as the one and only True Method. Let us not make the mistake of equating what they are doing with reason itself.

The mathematician Marston Morse once said, "The creative scientist lives in 'the wildness of logic' where reason is the handmaiden and not the master . . . I believe that it is only as an artist that man knows reality."[4]

Morse's conclusions, shared by many creative scientists often after long agony of introspection about how their discoveries were actually made, is that the logical, orderly, abstract processes of explicit reasoning are merely the surface manifestations of rationality. They presuppose other, less well-organized forms of experience which arise out of an immediacy of involvement, a total engagement of the mind and senses with the subject being studied. This type of involvement is the opposite of detachment and sequential logic. Without it, technical reason is doomed to perform its sterile operations in a vacuum. Reason is trivial when cut off from its grounds in direct experience.

The counterculture grasps this important truth, even though it chooses to ignore the complementary truth that direct experience undisciplined by technical reason can also be a treacherous master

---

[4] *Bulletin of the Atomic Scientists,* 15, p. 58, "Mathematics and the Arts." Quoted in Nisbet, *op. cit.,* p. 319.

leading to slovenly mysticism and ultimately to a breakdown of communication. Both forms of thought are as necessary to create understanding of reality as both sexes are needed to create new life.

In leaving this difficult subject without further discussion, I resign myself to inevitable misunderstanding. I have discussed it at great length elsewhere—469 pages worth—for those who have an interest in these arcane matters.[5]

The Sacred

The search for the sacred in nature—the third major theme in the cultural revolution's system of ideas—shares many of the same characteristics as the concern with reason and the nonrational. There is the same partial truth, the same unrealistic turning of one's back on what has already been accomplished—but also the same unerring aim at one of the most dangerous and critical imbalances in our American culture.

The point can be conveyed by contrasting a windmill with a bulldozer. The windmill has to accommodate itself to the wind and the terrain. To fulfill its function as a windmill it has to fit into a part of nature; it makes use of this region even as it accommodates itself to it. It also makes use of the wind. But it uses the wind in such a way as not to consume it. The wind continues on and remains the wind. The windmill can use the wind only by giving itself to it; it lets the wind be wind. In putting the wind to use, it does not suppress, repress, or otherwise level or convert the wind into something else.

The bulldozer is a human artifact of a very different kind. Its name conveys appropriately the idea of power: it does not accommodate itself to the objects of nature, but overpowers them. It bursts through obstacles, pushes them aside, levels them. The word "leveling" is significant here: as it levels, the bulldozer reduces trees, hills, and terrain into a uniform rubble. This rubble, of course, can become the side on which roads and houses are built. The human habitat is thus extended a little farther over the earth. All of this we unquestioningly call progress. The bulldozer has powers of transforming the conditions of life

---

[5] Daniel Yankelovich and William Barrett, *Ego and Instinct*. Vintage Books, 1971.

quite beyond the feeble achievements of the old-fashioned windmill.

But power is accompanied by responsibility. The uprooting of trees leads to soil erosion, inadequate drainage and easy flooding. A super-highway becomes a congested procession of automobiles and trucks belching fumes and noise. Nearby communities, which once had a life of their own, are transformed into mere traffic intersections. The bull-dozer has the power to create new conditions of life, but also to dis-rupt the whole fabric of life which already has a balance of its own. A fateful burden weighs upon the wisdom of the men who make use of it.

By contrast, a mistaken windmill has no such frightening possibil-ities. Perhaps the windmill has been put up in the wrong place to catch enough of the wind, or it is too far from the convenience of the neighboring farmers. But no permanent damage has been done. The mistakenly built windmill has not disrupted irreparably the life of the community around it. It need not even be taken down. It may be left where it is, an attractive though not very useful edifice gracing a land-scape. On the other hand, the consequences of the misuse of the bull-dozer are not so easily amended. In some cases, indeed, they might be irreparable. The windmill may well be a symbol of an archaic past—gentle, old-fashioned, and somewhat ineffectual; but the bulldozer is not necessarily a mark of progress in human evolution; and our human freedom does not consist in manipulating our natures and our environment any way we wish (as Sartre, Marx, and myriad other thinkers have urged).[6] Just as we should never use people merely as tools but regard them as ends in themselves, so now we must extend this moral imperative to nature. If human life is to be regarded as sacred, so is nature itself sacred. It cannot and must not be bulldozed into oblivion. Our very survival depends upon it not being bulldozed.

In summary, then, a preoccupation with nature and the natural, a tendency to romanticize nature, a striving to live in harmony with nature, an invidious contrasting of the virtues of natural man and the natural life with the corrupting influences of civilization—these are constant and recurring themes in Western intellectual history. But

---

[6] The description of the windmill and the bulldozer is from *Ego and Instinct*, pp. 459–60. I owe this striking contrast mainly to my co-author, William Barrett.

the stress on nature as it occurs in the student movement adds a vital new dimension to this tradition, one that cannot be dismissed as a mere romantic reaction to technological/materialist culture. It represents a basic shift in man's conception of himself and his place in the universe.

[III]

Having attempted to identify the essential idea implicit in the student movement, we are now in a better position to discuss some of the movement's forms of expression which are not authentic: they are the strange guises that, arising out of circumstances of the moment, are destined to fall by the wayside once these circumstances change. From the foregoing discussion of nature and the natural it should be clear that the great idea embodied in the student movement is *not* that of political revolution in the classic sense of an overt transfer of power from those who now wield it to those who carry out the revolution.

Since the early 1960's, the campus has served as incubator for two kinds of revolution—one political, the other cultural. Up to now, the two have interpenetrated each other, with the political side actually being the more prominent. Our research has shown that the tide of political radicalism shifted direction in 1971, receding somewhat from its 1970 high. Although the number of students who identify with the New Left has not diminished significantly over the past several years, the campus as a whole is far less politicized today than in previous years. The question now is, what will happen in the future? Will some new event such as a flare-up in Southeast Asia, a new political trial or a weakening of the economy rekindle radical political passions on campus? If a new charismatic leader suddenly appeared on the scene, could he readily convert student cynicism and frustration into renewed political commitment? Might a skillful shift in New Left tactics recapture the allegiance of the college student body or win adherents outside the campus—among blacks, Vietnam veterans, or unemployed workers? In short, has the thrust of campus-led political revolution merely paused before renewing itself, or has it entered a period of decline? How deep *are* the roots of student political radicalism?

Our interpretation of the student movement suggests that the campus-based political revolution is over for the foreseeable future, while the cultural revolution—the new naturalism—will continue to grow at an ever-increasing tempo. Undoubtedly, a cadre of political radicals will remain on campus—just as they have for decades. But as the cultural revolution gathers strength and spreads from the universities to the rest of the country, it will become increasingly evident that political radicalism is not what it is all about. The campus political movement of the late 1960's will turn out to be one of those strange guises assumed for a brief time by an idea whose destiny and pattern of unfolding lies elsewhere.

There are several reasons why the campus political revolution is losing momentum, one being that certain inherent contradictions between the two revolutions have begun to emerge. Up to now, such contradictions have been hidden from view. The prevailing assumption has been that the political and cultural elements belong together as expressions of a single revolutionary thrust. Indeed, New Left students who are most radical in their political views also find themselves in the vanguard of the cultural revolution. Observing this phenomenon, Jean-François Revel concludes (wrongly, we believe): "The moral, cultural and political revolutions are but a single revolution."[7] Revel and others underestimate the centrality of conflicts in values which, previously submerged, are slowly beginning to make themselves felt. Not surprisingly, the contradictions rise to the surface as student concepts of nature and the natural become clarified.

Consider, for example, the profoundly different conceptions of power and the role of power in each of the two idea systems. Those in the vanguard of the cultural revolution mistrust the use of power. They see power as a form of bulldozerism. They believe that transformations in people's basic values must take place without the need to employ coercive power because power destroys the very values they wish to advance. Peaceable revolution without the physical taking over of the power structure is the theme of two of the most influential books to have appeared in recent years: Charles Reich's *The Greening of America*,[8] and Revel's *Without Marx or Jesus*.[9] Writing from the perspective of a French intellectual, Revel's observations are par-

---

[7] *Saturday Review,* July 24, 1971, p. 17.

[8] Charles Reich, *The Greening of America*. Random House, 1970.

[9] Jean-François Revel, *Without Marx or Jesus*. Doubleday, 1971.

ticularly striking. Revel believes that a bloodless revolution in values is taking place in this country: "The revolution of the twentieth century will take place in the United States . . . it has already begun to develop there." Revel sees Cuba, China, and Russia as political revolutions that failed. He has in mind "a social, cultural, moral, even artistic transformation where the values of the old world are rejected, where relations between social classes are reconsidered, where relations among individuals are modified, where the concept of the family changes, where the value of work and the very goals of existence are reconsidered."[10]

Revel believes that the revolution began to emerge in the United States in the mid-1950's with the civil rights marches, and flowered in the student upheavals of the 1960's, in the black power movement, in Women's Liberation and in opposition to the Vietnam war.

Strikingly like Reich, Revel believes that fundamental changes are coming about in the United States more or less painlessly—that is, without political revolution—due to shifts in the value structure of the society. And he includes, particularly, that bastion of capitalist power, corporate industry. He states that value changes will permit industry to "preserve its dynamism while draining it of what is left of its capitalist control." Revel admits that this is perhaps a "slightly utopian scenario," but it is what he sees happening in the United States.

This prognosis of a peaceable revolution which leaves the Establishment in place and depends upon a belief that it is undergoing a spiritual transformation is emphatically not shared by campus radicals who hold a more traditional political view of the uses of power. The political revolutionary still thinks of power as flowing "from the barrel of a gun," and is prepared to draw upon the full repertory of political tactics for seizing power—confrontation, ideological indoctrination of the people, working from within, and if necessary, using violence to seize the instruments of power. Indeed, precisely because Reich has deemphasized these uses of power, Herbert Marcuse has attacked him for promoting a naive "Establishment version" of the revolution. Marcuse thinks it is silly and sentimental to conceive of those who

---

[10] *Ibid.*

hold power as surrendering to something as softheaded as a shift in consciousness.[11]

But Marcuse's emphasis on power is, in turn, troublesome to those who seek a cultural, moral, and aesthetic revolution. For these young people, the issue of power is also decisive, but in the very opposite sense. They mistrust power. They see the quest for power as one of the pernicious values of the society that must be uprooted. They identify the desire for power as destructive of the sense of community they deem so important. They see it as anti-egalitarian and unnatural.

Their deep mistrust of power draws on a long tradition. Psychologist Alfred Adler, writing in Germany in the early 1920's spoke of "this poison of craving for power." Anticipating the counterculture, he saw the quest for power as responsible for the destruction of all spontaneous human relationships. For Adler, the striving for power, especially personal power, is a "disastrous delusion." The simplest means to everything seems to be by way of power, but this "simplest means" always leads to destruction. All too often, the ideal of our times is the isolated hero for whom fellowmen are mere objects. The sickness of our civilization, in Adler's view, flows directly from the high valuation we place on power and on individualism at the expense of community.[12] Power, in other words, belongs with the despised and rejected idea system: individualism/egoism/manipulation-of-others/isolation/power. It is antithetical to the system: community/service/care-for-other/preservation-of-nature. The political revolutionary's preoccupation with power makes him, in effect, an enemy of the cultural revolution.

At the present time, both conceptions of revolution (political and cultural) and both conceptions of power (as the prize of political revolution and as the poison that eats away our sense of community and humanity) coexist without difficulty in the student movement. Yet the contradiction between the two conceptions could hardly be more fundamental. Up to now, it has been largely unconscious. But as it rises into consciousness it will force people to choose, and the process of

---

[11] Herbert Marcuse in *The New York Times*, November 6, 1970.
[12] Alfred Adler, "The Psychology of Power," in *Journal of Individual Psychology*, November 1966.

choice will inevitably drive a deep wedge between the two revolutions on campuses—to the disadvantage of the political revolution.

An Alien Ideology

There is a second reason for the decline of the political revolution on campus which is unrelated to student values. It has to do, simply and fundamentally, with the misfit between New Left ideology and American experience. Lacking essential relevance, the New Left is not likely to win enduring support among any large, significant group in the population—including the college student body itself.

Campus radicalism, represented by the New Left, has stressed several themes: our present social/political system is too rotten for repair and hence revolution is needed; power must be seized, peacefully if possible but violently if necessary; the real source of power in the country is vested in big business, our so-called democratic processes being a sham, a tool the moneyed interests manipulate to exploit various minorities in order to increase their wealth and privileges.

Stated in so bald and unadorned a fashion, this position in its entirety does not enjoy wide acceptance among college students. But it stands out as a prominent feature of the college movement for a number of reasons: the activist leadership of student strikes, protests, sit-ins, and confrontations have usually come from the New Left; the media, sensitized to political events, have played up the New Left as the most newsworthy part of the campus revolt. Most important of all, the war in Southeast Asia has caused millions of students to resonate sympathetically to the most severe criticisms of the society that they could find to listen to—and the New Left has obliged them. Furthermore, as the research so plainly shows, some elements of New Left ideology *are* shared by a majority of students, particularly those that echo a Marxist analysis of our institutions. Paradoxically, the college student mainstream is traditional in its basic life values, moderate in its prescriptions for change, but radical in its diagnosis of the society. The Marxist precept that economic power in a capitalistic society must control the political process dominates the campus view of the American political system.

Nor is this view confined to our colleges. It is widely held among certain minority groups and it has deep roots in the American Populist tradition with its long-standing mistrust of Wall Street and bigness in any form. It would take us too far afield to discuss at length the accuracy of this Marxist premise. But since the question of its accuracy is pivotal, some comment, however brief, must be made.

If big business is, indeed, the main locus of political power in our society, then the political revolution does have some chance to succeed. Eventually, it can learn how to channel the widespread dissatisfaction that exists in the country, particularly among huge and potentially powerful minority groups, ethnic groups, the poor, the undereducated and underpaid, and paradoxically, the overeducated and overpaid as well. If poverty can be eliminated, racism overcome, peace secured, freedom guaranteed, affluence spread, the blight of the cities arrested, crime and drug abuse stopped, and fraternal brotherhood created by smashing the power of big business, then the revolution is still in business. But if the political power of business in our mixed economy is, in fact, far more limited than its opponents believe; if political power actually resides in the political process itself, where, in theory, it is supposed to reside (and that process is clogged, not by business but by archaic forms of governmental organization); if the society as a whole is too damn complicated to be explained by a nineteenth-century slogan concerning the nature of European capitalism, then the New Left is looking up the wrong tree—which is precisely what I believe it is doing.

Arthur Schlesinger, Jr., has stated the central point: "The history of twentieth-century thought is a record of the manifold ways in which humanity has been betrayed by ideology. . . . Much of the world today is oppressed by the insistence that it must choose between 'capitalism' and 'socialism.' Yet, the rise in the last generation of the mixed society —of the view that it is possible to give the state sufficient power to bring about social welfare and economic growth without thereby giving it power to abolish political and civic freedom—has revealed classical capitalism and classical socialism as nineteenth-century doctrines, left behind by the onward rush of science and technology. The world has moved beyond these obsolete ideologies toward a far more subtle and flexible social strategy. It is evident now, for example, that the choice between private and public means, that choice which has obsessed so much recent political and economic discussion in under-developed countries, is not a matter of religious principle. It is not a moral issue to be decided on absolutist grounds either by those on the right who regard the use of public means as wicked and sinful, or by those on the left who regard the use of private means as wicked and sinful . . . It is a problem to be answered not by theology but by experience and experiment. Indeed, I would suggest that we banish the words 'capitalism' and 'socialism' from intellectual discourse. These words no longer have clear meanings. They are sources of heat, not of light. They belong to the vocabulary of demagoguery, not to the vocabulary of analysis."[13]

As the late economist, Joseph Schumpeter, cagily observed a number of years ago, when one turns from hard to soft property, the transition to socialism will never even be noticed.

I am not implying here that big business in the United States is not a powerful force, which it clearly is, or that far-reaching changes in business's relation to society are not in order, which they are. Nor do I wish to oversimplify the doctrines of New Left writers, some of whom bring an acute and subtle intelligence to bear on our problems. I confine myself here to one essential point: namely, that the version of Marxism, as held by the mass of students and applied by them to our contemporary American society, is steeped in invincible ignorance and will neither yield productive insights nor produce effective programs for social change.

It is surely one of the scandals of American intellectual life that no explanatory theory of how our society works is able to compete on campus in its power of generality and persuasiveness with warmed-over Marxism. Generation after generation of college students pick up, almost by osmosis, the compelling but false picture of our society generated by a vulgarized Marxism.

Conservatives like to blame radical professors for this state of affairs. Actually, the cause goes much deeper. In our colleges theories of all kinds are kept alive. By and large, they are gloriously eclectic. But our leadership groups outside of the academic community reject virtually *all* forms of theory. For all practical purposes, we have no widely accepted theory of the contemporary American political/eco-

---

[13] Arthur Schlesinger, Jr., "The One and the Many," in Schlesinger and White, *Currents in American Thought*, p. 536.

nomic system. Despite the thousands of books, there is want in the midst of plenty.

And so we arrive at an impasse. Without a valid diagnosis of American experience, the New Left will win no lasting following among the public at large; their student supporters will continue to turn away from them to pursue less frustrating pastimes, and the point of view they represent will confine itself to a small isolated minority.

Paradoxically, the practical men of affairs are caught in a similar bind. Lacking a sound theory of the American social system, many a battle will be fought over the wrong issues by the wrong people with an inconclusive outcome. Radical students will continue to shout Marxist slogans; conservative businessmen will go on grumbling about radical professors; politicians will continue to make political hay out of belaboring the power of big business while simultaneously criticizing business for not doing more for the community (i.e., assuming even more power). And all the while, our political and economic life will move on, its direction shaped by other forces.

Among the most potent of these other forces will be the real student revolution—the changing conception of man's relationship to a nature that is no longer seen as infinite, brutish, and something to be mastered with the bulldozer, but as finite, precious, fragile, and essentially good. We are being asked to stop our frantic rush to bend nature to the human will and instead to restore a vital, more harmonious—and more humble—balance with nature.

APPENDIX

Technical Details
of
the Survey

The Sample

The 1971 Yankelovich campus study was based on a total of 1,244 interviews completed at 50 colleges.

Selection of the Institutions

The sampling procedures paralleled those used in the 1968, 1969, and 1970 studies.

The sampling universe covered all colleges (both two- and four-year) and universities in the United States. The institutions were first stratified by four regions. Within each region, a second stratification was based on whether the institution was public or private. Within each of the final strata, the institutions were then arrayed by size—starting with the smallest enrollment up to the largest. Final selection of the colleges and universities was then picked randomly within each stratification.

Selection of the Respondents

At each institution, quotas were established for "year of college" (freshman, sophomore, junior, senior), sex, and race, based on the characteristics of the school's population. All quotas based on individual schools' populations were then pro-rated to national figures.[1]

_____

[1] *Source: Digest of Education Statistics.* Published by the U.S. Department of Health, Education, and Welfare.

At each school, a random selection procedure was controlled within each quota breakdown by assignment of numbers of persons whose last names began with specific letters of the alphabet. This procedure insured that the final selection of respondents would be truly random —and not biased by interviewing procedures.

Characteristics of the 1971 Sample

Sex
Male	52
Female	48

Age
17–19	33
20–21	33
22–23	18
24 plus	16

Marital Status
Single	83
Married	16
Widowed, divorced, separated	1

Race
White	87
Non-white	13

Religion
Protestant	41
Catholic	21
Jewish	8
Other	8
None	21

The following are the sampling points for the four surveys:

1968 Sampling Points

Amherst College
Arizona State University
University of Arkansas
Asheville-Biltmore College
University of California (Berkeley)
Central State University, Ohio
Del-Mar College
Delta College
Elmira College
Furman University
George Washington University
Georgia State College
Hanover College
Harvard University
Kansas State University
Los Angeles City College

McNeese State College
University of Minnesota
University of Missouri
Nassau Community College, New York
University of Nebraska
University of Pittsburgh
Portland State College, Oregon
University of Rhode Island
Rio Hondo Junior College
University of Rochester
St. Gregory's College, Oklahoma
University of Wisconsin (Superior)
Walla Walla College
Western Washington State College

1969 Sampling Points

Amherst College
Arizona State University
University of Arkansas
Asheville-Biltmore College
University of California (Berkeley)
Central State University, Ohio
Del-Mar College
Delta College
Elmira College
Furman University
George Washington University
Georgia State College
Hanover College
Harvard University
Kansas State University
Los Angeles City College

McNeese State College
University of Minnesota
University of Missouri
Nassau Community College, New York
University of Nebraska
University of Pittsburgh
Portland State College, Oregon
University of Rhode Island
Rio Hondo Junior College
University of Rochester
St. Gregory's College, Oklahoma
University of Wisconsin (Superior)
Walla Walla College
Western Washington State College

1970 Sampling Points

State University of New York
(Albany)
Boston University
Brigham Young University
Columbia University
Dillard University
University of Florida
Fresno State College
Furman University
Georgetown College
Harvard University

Howard University
Ithaca College
Kansas State University
Luther College
Miami University (Ohio)
University of Nebraska
Ohio State University
University of Oklahoma
San Diego State College
Smith College
Wisconsin State University

1971 Sampling Points

Arkansas State University
Armstrong State College
City University of New York
(Baruch)
University of California (Berkeley)
Boston University
Brigham Young University
Bronx Community College
State University of New York
(Buffalo)
Cedarville College
Central Connecticut State College
Central Michigan University
Chicago City College
University of Connecticut
Creighton University
Emory University
Fullerton Junior College
Genesee Community College
University of Georgia
Georgia State University
Golden West College

Indiana University
Iowa State University of Science
and Technology
Jackson State Community College
University of Kansas
Lebanon Valley College
Lehigh University
Long Beach City College
Marshall University
Michigan Tech University
University of Missouri
Mt. San Antonio College
Nevada Southern University
College of New Rochelle
Northeastern Junior College
Northern Arizona University
North Texas State University
Pasadena City College
Long Island University (C. W.
Post)
University of Puget Sound
Purdue University

Riverside City College
Rockhurst College
Rutgers University
St. Cloud State College
St. Johns College

South Carolina State College
University of Tennessee
Troy State College
Virginia Polytech
Washington University, Missouri

Here are reproductions of the questionnaires used in interviewing the 1,244 students. Each interview lasted approximately one hour.

Daniel Yankelovich, Inc.
575 Madison Avenue
New York, New York 10022

Job #8885   1-
April, 1971   2-
               3-
               4-

1971 COLLEGE YOUTH STUDY

CLASSIFICATION DATA

	5-	6-	7-	8-	9-	10-

Name of Respondent:_____ C.F. No.:

College:_____

College Address:_____City:_____State:_____

Telephone No.:_____

Home Address:_____City:_____State:_____

Telephone No.:_____

Interviewer:_____Date:_____

A. Sex:
   Male.........................11-1
   Female...................... -2

B. Age:
   17 years old.................12-1
   18 years old................ -2
   19 years old................ -3
   20 years old................ -4
   21 years old................ -5
   22 years old................ -6
   23 years old................ -7
   24 years or older........... -8

C. Marital Status:
   Married....................13-1
   Single...................... -2
   Other....................... -3

D. Respondent's Occupational Status:
   Employed full time..........14-1
   Employed part time.......... -2
   Not employed................ -3

E. Own Income (If Employed):
   (SHOW CARD S)
   Under $1,000 per year.......15-1
   $1,000 - 2,999 per year..... -2
   $3,000 - 4,999 per year..... -3
   $5,000 and over per year.... -4

F. Parents' Education:

	Mother	Father
High school or less....	16-1	17-1
Some college...........	-2	-2
College graduate.......	-3	-3
Post-graduate..........	-4	-4

G. Father's Occupation:
   Professional/executive/
     managerial................18-1
   White collar................ -2
   Blue collar................. -3
   Other....................... -4

H. Parent's Income: (SHOW CARD T)
   Under $3,000 per year.......19-1
   $3,000 - 4,999 per year..... -2
   $5,000 - 9,999 per year... -3
   $10,000 - 14,999 per year... -4
   $15,000 or more per year.... -5

I. Race (BY OBSERVATION):
   White.......................20-1
   Black....................... -2
   Puerto Rican................ -3
   Mexican..................... -4

   Other:_____ -5
         (SPECIFY)

J. Year of College Attending:
   One (Freshman)..............21-1
   Two (Sophomore)............. -2
   Three (Junior).............. -3
   Four (Senior)............... -4
   Five (Graduate)............. -5

K. Major:
   Humanities/social science,
     psychology................22-1
   Education................... -2
   Science/mathematics......... -3
   Engineering................. -4
   Business.................... -5
   Undecided/don't know........ -6

   Other:_____ -7
         (SPECIFY)

L. Do you expect to complete your
   studies and get your degree?
             (ASK M) - Yes.........23-1
   (SKIP TO N) ⟨ No.......... -2
               ⟨ Not sure..... -3

M. (IF NOT GRADUATE STUDENT) Do
   you expect to go to graduate
   school?
                        Yes.....24-1
                        No...... -2

194

N. Which political party do you
identify with most closely?
Democrat....................25-1
Republican.................. -2
Other:_____ -3
          (SPECIFY)
None........................ -4

O. Are you registered to vote?
Registered.................26-1
Not registered............. -2

P. (IF NOT) Do you plan to
register for the 1972
elections?
Yes........................27-1
No.......................... -2

Q. (IF REGISTERED OR PLAN TO
REGISTER) Do you expect to
cast your vote in the 1972
elections?
Yes........................28-1
No.......................... -2

R. (SHOW CARD U) Regardless of
any party affiliation, do you
think of yourself as:
Conservative...............29-1
Moderate/conservative...... -2
Moderate/middle of the
   road..................... -3
Liberal/middle of the
   road..................... -4
Liberal.................... -5
Radical.................... -6

S. What is your religious
preference?
Protestant.................30-1
Catholic.................... -2
Jewish..................... -3
Other...................... -4
None....................... -5

T. (SHOW CARD V) Here are two
statements made by college
students on their reasons for
going to college. Please indicate which statement comes
closest to your own views--
even if neither of them fits
exactly.
Statement F................31-1
Statement G................ -2

U. (IF MALE) What is your draft
Callup Number?
Under 100..................32-1
100 - 200.................. -2
200 and over............... -3
1Y......................... -4
4F......................... -5
CO......................... -6
Already served............. -7

APPENDIX

We're conducting a study among college students and I'd like to ask you some questions about yourself and your attitudes toward some of the important questions of the day.

==
I - THE ISSUES
==

1a. Generally how do you feel that things are going in the country today--very well, fairly well, pretty badly, or very badly?

```
                                          Very well........33-1
                                          Fairly well......  -2
                                          Pretty badly.....  -3
                                          Very badly.......  -4
                                          Not sure.........  -5
```

b. Do you think that:

	Yes	No	Not Sure
The war in Vietnam will be over by the next presidential election?	34-1	-2	-3
Economic conditions in the country will improve this year?	35-1	-2	-3

c. (HAND CARD A) Which of these phrases best describes your own current mood and state of mind? CALL OFF THE LETTER AND NAME AS MANY AS APPLY.

```
        a.  Happy...........................36-1
        b.  Serene...........................  -2
        c.  Disgusted........................  -3
        d.  Withdrawn........................  -4

        e.  Angry............................  -5
        f.  Confused about the future.......  -6
        g.  Stimulated.......................  -7
        h.  Quiet............................  -8

        i.  Encouraged.......................  -9
        j.  Discouraged......................  -0
        k.  Weary............................  -x
        l.  Optimistic about the future.....  -y

        m.  Agitated.........................37-1
        n.  Full of hate and violence.......  -2
        o.  Apathetic........................  -3
        p.  Involved.........................  -4

        q.  Depressed........................  -5
        r.  Satisfied........................  -6
        s.  Worried..........................  -7
        t.  Bored............................  -8

        u.  Frustrated.......................  -9
        v.  Cynical..........................  -0
        w.  Skeptical........................  -x
            None.............................  -y
            Not sure.........................  -z
```

196

TECHNICAL DETAILS OF THE SURVEY

1d.   I'd like to ask you to contrast your present mood with how you felt last spring. For example, are you more (**READ LIST**) now than you were last year, less, or about the same?

	More Now	Less Now	About the Same
Involved in your own private life and concerns......	38-1	-2	-3
Serious about studying.............................	39-1	.-2	-3
Discouraged about the chances for bringing about desired changes in the society......................	40-1	-2	-3
Radical in your political thinking..................	41-1	-2	-3
Close to your family...............................	42-1	-2	-3
Angry and determined to do something...............	43-1	-2	-3
Concerned about what is happening in Vietnam........	44-1	-2	-3
Involved in working for change.....................	45-1	-2	-3
Fearful about being able to get a job in the future...	46-1	-2	-3
Accepting of violence as a legitimate tactic to achieve desired social change......................	47-1	-2	-3
Fearful of repression..............................	48-1	-2	-3
Willing to participate in protests.................	49-1	-2	-3
Confident about which tactics are right and effective in achieving change......................	50-1	-2	-3
Convinced about the impotence and powerlessness of individuals like yourself to effect change..........	51-1	-2	-3
Alienated from the society.........................	52-1	-2	-3
Interested in working in political campaigns........	53-1	-2	-3
Confident about the underlying health of the country...	54-1	-2	-3
Conservative in your political thinking.............	55-1	-2	-3
Happy in your own personal life....................	56-1	-2	-3
Skeptical of the truthfulness of government leaders...	57-1	-2	-3

197

2a.　(SHOW CARD B)　Which two or three problems or issues facing the country concern you personally the most?　(RECORD IN 2a BELOW)

b.　Would you be willing to make a personal commitment such as devoting a year or two of your life to doing something about any of these issues?　Which ones?　(RECORD IN 2b BELOW)

	2a Feel Most Strongly About	2b Make a Commitment
Bringing peace in Vietnam.........................	58-1	61-1
Curbing inflation................................	-2	-2
Limiting the arms race...........................	-3	-3
Fighting poverty.................................	-4	-4
Controlling population...........................	-5	-5
Winning women's rights...........................	-6	-6
Combating racism.................................	-7	-7
Fighting pollution...............................	-8	-8
Defending consumers' rights......................	59-1	62-1
Bringing peace to the Middle East................	-2	-2
Reforming our political institutions.............	-3	-3
Helping the third world..........................	-4	-4
Changing the social system.......................	-5	-5
Legalizing marijuana.............................	-6	-6
Legalizing abortions in every state..............	-7	-7
Combating crime..................................	-8	-8
Reducing hard drug addiction.....................	60-1	63-1
Reforming the courts and judicial system.........	-2	-2
Aid to higher education..........................	-3	-3
Revenue sharing..................................	-4	-4
Welfare reform...................................	-5	-5
Not willing to make a commitment.................	-6	xx

c.　If you were to commit yourself to this type of activity, would you sooner work as part of a protest movement or part of the establishment?

```
                                        Protest...........64-1
                                        Establishment.....  -2
                                        No difference.....  -3
                                        Neither...........  -4
```

d.　If you had to choose, whom would you most prefer to work with jointly on this type of activity?　(READ LIST)

```
        Business leaders...............................................65-1
        Members of the executive branch of the federal government.....  -2
        Federal agencies and departments..............................  -3
        Members of Congress...........................................  -4
        Candidates for political office...............................  -5
        Community leaders and civic groups............................  -6
        State government..............................................  -7
        Federal government............................................  -8

        Other (SPECIFY):_____

        _____

        None of these.................................................  -x
```

===
II - THE WAR
===

3a.   Most people agree that we should get out of Vietnam--but there are
      different views about how and when we should leave. Here are some of
      the most current views. (HAND CARD C) Which one view most closely
      resembles your own viewpoint?

    A.   We must first insure a noncommunist government in
       South Vietnam..66-1

    B.   We must first have an orderly transfer of responsi-
       bility from United States troops to the South
       Vietnamese... -2

    C.   We should leave now.. -3

    D.   None of these (PLEASE SPECIFY YOUR VIEWS)................. -4

    _____67-

b.   Some people have felt that student opposition to the invasion of Laos
      was considerably less vigorous and vocal than to the Cambodia invasion
      a year ago. Has this been true around here?

            (ASK Q.3c) - True.........68-1
                          Not true..... -2
            (SKIP TO Q.4a)<
                          Not sure..... -3

c.   (HAND CARD D) Which of these statements do you feel best accounts for
      the difference in the campus response to Laos?

    A.   Students wanted to see if the President was right--and
       that this was a way to shorten the war and our involvement.....69-1

    B.   Students are tired of protesting and rallying because they
       have learned that the government doesn't listen, and it
       has no results... -2

    C.   There is no real antiwar leadership on the campus at the
       present time... -3

    D.   Students are so sickened by the war and turned off by our
       society that they have just withdrawn from the rest of
       the nation... -4

    E.   It was late in starting, but there will be mounting
       protest now that spring is here............................... -5

    F.   With the economy the way it is, students are worried about
       their future and are concentrating on their studies........... -6

    Other (SPECIFY):_____

    _____

    Not sure.. -x

4a.   (SHOW CARD E) What is your own moral position as far as the Vietnam
      war is concerned? For example, in instances such as the Mylai
      affair, who do you think must be held responsible? (MULTIPLE RECORD)

      The individual soldier or officer, such as Lieutenant Calley......70-1
      The commanding officer... -2
      The United States general in charge of the campaign............... -3
      The Secretary of Defense.. -4
      The President of the United States................................ -5
      We are all responsible.. -6
      This kind of thing is inevitable and no one is responsible........ -7

  b.   If the Vietnam war was to end today, do you feel that we could look
       forward to a period of peace, or do you feel similar future involve-
       ments are almost inevitable as a result of our present policies?

                        Peace....................................71-1
                        Similar military future involvements..... -2
                        Not sure/depends......................... -3

  c.   (HAND CARD F) In your opinion, where do you feel the real power in
       this country is vested?

                Congress.......................................72-1
                The President.................................... -2
                The giant corporations.......................... -3
                The Defense Department.......................... -4

                CIA... -5
                The general public............................. -6
                The Democratic party........................... -7
                The Republican party........................... -8

                Financiers and financial institutions......... -9
                The technocrats................................ -0
                The interplay of diverse special interests group, such
                    as labor, religious leaders and educators................ -x
                Other.. -y

                Not sure....................................... -z

                                                              80-1

CARD II

III - SOCIETY

5a.   Some people are calling this country a "sick society." Do you agree
      or disagree with them?
                                              Agree......... 5-1
                                              Disagree...... -2
                                              Not sure...... -3

200

TECHNICAL DETAILS OF THE SURVEY

5b. (HAND WHITE DECK OF CARDS) Here's a deck of cards that lists some of the factors people have mentioned as significant indications that things are not working properly today. Will you go through the deck and put into one pile just the really serious indications that things are not working as far as you are concerned.

Serious
Indications
(PLEASE
CIRCLE)

1.	Vietnam war.....................................	6-1
2.	Racial prejudice...............................	-2
3.	Poverty..	-3
4.	The deterioration of the cities...............	-4
5.	Commercialism..................................	-5
6.	Pollution......................................	-6
7.	The depletion of natural resources............	-7
8.	Lack of long-range planning....................	-8
9.	Declining public services.....................	-9
10.	Low voter turnout..............................	-0
11.	Rising crime rate..............................	7-1
12.	Polarization...................................	-2
13.	Corruption.....................................	-3
14.	Drug addiction.................................	-4
15.	Treatment of the aged..........................	-5
16.	The quality of life............................	-6
17.	Lack of concern................................	-7
18.	The emphasis on money..........................	-8
19.	The concentration of wealth....................	-9
20.	Emphasis on technology.........................	-0
21.	Lack of social justice.........................	8-1
22.	The crackdown on dissent.......................	-2
23.	The generation gap.............................	-3
24.	The profit motive..............................	-4
25.	Lack of leadership.............................	-5
26.	Wiretapping....................................	-6
27.	The power of the industrial-military complex........	-7
28.	Decline in religion............................	-8
29.	The cultural shock.............................	-9
30.	Decline of sexual morality.....................	-0
31.	Failure of local government to keep pace with change....	9-1
32.	Dependence on government handouts..............	-2
33.	Erosion of respect for authority..............	-3
34.	Excessive influence of mass media.............	-4
35.	Emphasis on pornography........................	-5
36.	Decline in civility...........................	-6
37.	Erosion of civil liberties....................	-7
38.	Amount of waste and spending..................	-8
	None of these.................................	-9
	All of these..................................	-0

201

6. (SHOW CARD G) This card lists a number of criticisms that have been made in recent years about American society. For each one, will you tell me whether you strongly agree, partially agree, or whether you strongly disagree. (ONE ANSWER FOR EACH STATEMENT)

	Strongly Agree	Partially Agree	Strongly Disagree
1. Our foreign policy is based on our own narrow economic and power interests........	10-1	-2	-3
2. Business is overly concerned with profits and not with public responsibility.........	11-1	-2	-3
3. The individual in today's society is isolated and cut off from meaningful relationships with others.................	12-1	-2	-3
4. There is more concern today for the 'welfare bum" who doesn't want to work than for the hard working person who is struggling to make a living...............	13-1	-2	-3
5. Economic well-being in this country is unjustly and unfairly distributed..........	14-1	-2	-3
6. Basically we are a racist nation...........	15-1	-2	-3
7. Morally and spiritually our country has lost its way..............................	16-1	-2	-3
8. The war in Vietnam is pure imperialism.....	17-1	-2	-3
9. Today's American society is characterized by 'injustice, insensitivity, lack of candor and inhumanity."...................	18-1	-2	-3
10. There is too much concern with equality and too little with law and order..........	19-1	-2	-3
11. Computers and other advanced technology are creating an inhuman and impersonal world..	20-1	-2	-3
12. The "Establishment" unfairly controls every aspect of our lives. We can never be free until we are rid of it.............	21-1	-2	-3
13. The present two party system does not offer any real alternatives................	22-1	-2	-3
14. A minority must never be allowed to impose its will on the majority............	23-1	-2	-3
15. Police should not hesitate to use force to maintain order..........................	24-1	-2	-3
16. People's 'privacy" is being destroyed......	25-1	-2	-3
17. Representative democracy can respond effectively to the needs of the people.....	26-1	-2	-3
18. A mass revolutionary party should be created..................................	27-1	-2	-3
19. Radicals of the left are as much a threat to the rights of the individual as are radicals of the right..............	28-1	-2	-3
20. You can never achieve freedom within the framework of contemporary American society..	29-1	-2	-3
21. No one should be punished for violating a law which he feels is immoral............	30-1	-2	-3

7a   How well do you feel that social justice functions in this country? For instance, do you think that (READ LIST) can be assured of a fair trial and judicial process?

	Yes	No	Not Sure
Conscientious objectors.................	31-1	-2	-3
Black Panthers.........................	32-1	-2	-3
College protesters.....................	33-1	-2	-3
American Indians.......................	34-1	-2	-3
Middle class blacks....................	35-1	-2	-3
Weathermen.............................	36-1	-2	-3
Dissenting servicemen..................	37-1	-2	-3
Antiwar leaders........................	38-1	-2	-3
Drug pushers...........................	39-1	-2	-3
Strike leaders.........................	40-1	-2	-3
Radicals...............................	41-1	-2	-3
Manufacturers of defective products.....	42-1	-2	-3
Polluters..............................	43-1	-2	-3
Petty criminals........................	44-1	-2	-3
Prostitutes............................	45-1	-2	-3
Homosexuals............................	46-1	-2	-3
Drug addicts...........................	47-1	-2	-3
Mexican Americans......................	48-1	-2	-3
Members of the Klan....................	49-1	-2	-3
Student activists......................	50-1	-2	-3
Landlords..............................	51-1	-2	-3
Tax evaders............................	52-1	-2	-3
Members of the "mob" underworld.........	53-1	-2	-3
War criminals..........................	54-1	-2	-3

b.   Generally do you think of (READ LIST) as being members of an oppressed or discriminated group in our society or not?

	Yes	No	Not Sure
Women.................	55-1	-2	-3
Hard Hats.............	56-1	-2	-3
Long Hairs............	57-1	-2	-3
Homosexuals...........	58-1	-2	-3
The blacks............	59-1	-2	-3
The poor..............	60-1	-2	-3
College students......	61-1	-2	-3
American Indians......	62-1	-2	-3
Mexican Americans.....	63-1	-2	-3
White southerners.....	64-1	-2	-3
High school dropouts..	65-1	-2	-3

APPENDIX

8.   (HAND CARD H) Which one of the descriptions on this card do you feel
      best describes each of the following institutions?

	Viable/ Needs No Substantial Change	Needs Moderate Change	Needs Fundamental Change	Should Be Done Away With
Big business.............	66-1	-2	-3	-4
The military..............	67-1	-2	-3	-4
The trade unions..........	68-1	-2	-3	-4
The political parties.....	69-1	-2	-3	-4
The mass media............	70-1	-2	-3	-4
Congress..................	71-1	-2	-3	-4
The FBI...................	72-1	-2	-3	-4
The Supreme Court.........	73-1	-2	-3	-4
The penal system..........	74-1	-2	-3	-4
The constitution..........	75-1	-2	-3	-4
Universities..............	76-1	-2	-3	-4
Foundations...............	77-1	-2	-3	-4

80-2

CARD III

9a.   (SHOW CARD I) Which one of the following views of American society
      and American life best reflects your own feelings? (SINGLE ANSWER)

      A   The American way of life is superior to that of any
           other country.. 5-1

      B.   There are serious flaws in our society today but the
           system is flexible enough to solve them.................. -2

      C.   The American system is not flexible enough, radical
           change is needed... -3

      D.   The whole social system ought to be replaced by an
           entirely new one. The existing structures are too
           rotten for repair.. -4

   b.   Which of these values do you believe are worth fighting a war for,
        which do you believe are not worth fighting a war for, and for which
        would you say it depends on the special circumstances? (READ LIST)

		Worth Fighting	Not Worth Fighting	Depends
a.	Keeping a commitment..................	6-1	-2	-3
b.	Containing the communists.............	7-1	-2	-3
c.	Maintaining our position of power in the world	8-1	-2	-3
d.	Protecting allies.....................	9-1	-2	-3
e.	Fighting for our honor	10-1	-2	-3
f.	Counteracting aggression..............	11-1	-2	-3
g.	Protecting our national interests.....	12-1	-2	-3

204

IV - SOCIAL INSTITUTIONS AND VALUES

10a. Many people feel that we are undergoing a period of rapid social change in this country today, and that people's values are changing at the same time. Which of the following changes would you __welcome__, which would you __reject__ and which would leave you __indifferent__? (READ LIST)

	Welcome	Reject	Indifferent
Less emphasis on money.....................	13-1	-2	-3
Less emphasis on working hard.............	14-1	-2	-3
More emphasis on law and order.............	15-1	-2	-3
More emphasis on technological improvement.............................	16-1	-2	-3
More emphasis on self-expression...........	17-1	-2	-3
More acceptance of sexual freedom..........	18-1	-2	-3
Less difference between the sexes..........	19-1	-2	-3
More emphasis on ethnic identification.....	20-1	-2	-3
More emphasis on religious beliefs.........	21-1	-2	-3
More emphasis on black power..............	22-1	-2	-3
More emphasis on friendliness and neighborliness...........................	23-1	-2	-3
More acceptance of homosexuals.............	24-1	-2	-3
More emphasis on group living.............	25-1	-2	-3
More emphasis on pleasure..................	26-1	-2	-3
More emphasis on psychotherapy.............	27-1	-2	-3
More respect for authority.................	28-1	-2	-3
More emphasis on traditional family ties...	29-1	-2	-3

b. What role does each of the following values play in your life--is it very important to you, fairly important, or not very important to you? (READ LIST)

	Very Important	Fairly Important	Not Very Important
Friendship....................	30-1	-2	-3
Money........................	31-1	-2	-3
Beauty.......................	32-1	-2	-3
Love.........................	33-1	-2	-3
Privacy......................	34-1	-2	-3
Expressing your opinion.......	35-1	-2	-3
Patriotism...................	36-1	-2	-3
Religion.....................	37-1	-2	-3
Living a clean moral life.....	38-1	-2	-3
Doing things for others.......	39-1	-2	-3
Changing society..............	40-1	-2	-3
Work.........................	41-1	-2	-3
Education....................	42-1	-2	-3
Being close to nature.........	43-1	-2	-3
Family.......................	44-1	-2	-3
Being creative...............	45-1	-2	-3
Not compromising beliefs......	46-1	-2	-3
Comfort......................	47-1	-2	-3

205

APPENDIX

11. Now I'm going to read you a list of statements which represent some
     traditional American values. I'd like you to tell me for each one
     whether you personally <u>believe</u> or <u>don't believe</u> in it. For example,
     do you believe or not believe that:

	Believe	Don't Believe
Hard work will always pay off......................	48-1	49-1
Everyone should save as much money as he can regularly and not have to lean on family and friends the minute he runs into financial problems..	-2	-2
Depending on how much strength and character a person has, he can pretty well control what happens to him.......................................	-3	-3
Belonging to some organized religion is important in a person's life..................................	-4	-4
Commitment to a meaningful career is a very important part of a person's life...................	-5	-5
Competition encourages excellence...................	-6	-6
The right to private property is sacred............	-7	-7
Society needs some legally based authority in order to prevent chaos..............................	-8	-8
Anyone who violates the law for reasons of conscience should be willing to accept the legal consequences..	-9	-9
Business is entitled to make a profit..............	-0	-0
Children should respect their parents..............	-x	-x
Duty before pleasure...............................	-y	-y

12a. Which of the following activities do you feel are morally wrong from
      your personal point of view, and which do you feel are not a moral
      issue? (READ LIST)

	Morally Wrong	Not a Moral Issue
Destroying private property...........................	50-1	51-1
Having an abortion....................................	-2	-2
Relations between consenting homosexuals..............	-3	-3
Casual sexual relations...............................	-4	-4
Planning and having children without formal marriage...	-5	-5
Collecting welfare when you could work................	-6	-6
Interchanging partners among couples..................	-7	-7
Breaking the law......................................	-8	-8
Leaving the country to avoid the draft................	-9	-9
Extra-marital sexual relations........................	-0	-0
Taking things without paying for them.................	-x	-x
Paying one's way through college by selling dope.......	-y	-y

12b. Some people have said that the present institution of marriage is becoming obsolete. Do you agree or disagree?

                                        Agree........52-1
                                        Disagree..... -2

13a. How do you feel about the criticism that the traditional family structure of mother, father and children living under one roof no longer works? Do you agree or disagree with the critics?

                                        Agree........53-1
                                        Disagree..... -2
                                        Not sure..... -3

b. Do you look forward to the idea of being legally married?

                        Look forward......................54-1
                        Don't look forward................ -2
                        Already married (volunteered)..... -3
                        Not sure.......................... -4

c. Are you interested in having children?

                                        Yes..........55-1
                                        No........... -2
                                        Not sure..... -3

d. Many young people today are living in collectives or communes. Is this something that would interest you on a short term commitment, such as a few years, as a permanent way of life, or not at all?

                                        Short term.....56-1
                                        Permanent...... -2
                                        Not at all..... -3
                                        Not sure....... -4

e. One hears more and more about groups of young people going off to live off the land and settling in small agricultural and rural areas. Is this something that would interest you for a year or two, would you welcome it as a permanent way of life, or doesn't the idea have any appeal for you at all?

                                        Year or two.....57-1
                                        Permanent....... -2
                                        No appeal....... -3
                                        Not sure........ -4

f. Do you feel an individual who believes in changing society can do more by living "outside" the traditional social structure or by working from "within"?

                                        Outside......58-1
                                        Within....... -2
                                        Not sure..... -3

207

14a. (SHOW CARD J) Which of these phrases best describes your own feelings?
(CHOOSE AS MANY AS YOU WISH)

    1. I would like just about the same kind of life for my-
        self as my parents have had................................59-1

    2. I anticipate no great difficulty in accepting the kind
        of life the society has to offer--a good job, marriage,
        children, living in a pleasant community and becoming
        part of that community................................... -2

    3. It's not going to be easy for me to accept the con-
        ventional job/marriage/children/home of your own, kind
        of life, but I don't see any other alternative........... -3

    4. I find the prospect of accepting a conventional way of
        life in the society as it now exists intolerable......... -4

  b. Is there any other country or society that you think you might prefer
      to live in?

                                   (ASK Q.14c) - Yes..........60-1
                            (SKIP TO Q.15a) < No........... -2
                                               Not sure..... -3

  c. Which society or country would that be?

                                                                61-

                                                                62-

---

V - WORK AND CAREER

15a. (HAND CARD K) Which of the considerations on this card will have a
      relatively strong influence on your choice of career? (MULTIPLE
      RECORD)

              Your family.......................................63-1
              The chance to get ahead........................... -2
              The money you can earn............................ -3
              The prestige or status of the job................. -4
              The security of the job........................... -5

              The ability to express yourself................... -6
              The challenge of the job.......................... -7
              The opportunity to make a meaningful contribution. -8
              Free time to pursue outside interests............. -9
              Offers the opportunity to work with other people rather
                 than to manipulate them........................ -0

              Other (SPECIFY):_____ -x

              I have no intention of pursuing a career.......... -y

                                                                64-

                                  208

15b. Do you have any doubts about being able to make as much money as you
may want to--whatever that amount is?

                                        Yes.....65-1
                                        No...... -2

 c. Do you have any doubts about your ability to be successful as you
 define success?

                                        Yes..... -3
                                        No...... -4

 d. (HAND CARD L) Which of the following do you think could be barriers
 towards getting the kind of work you want?

                    Your race...........................66-1
                    Your religion........................ -2
                    Your sex............................. -3
                    Your family background.............. -4
                    Your style of dress................. -5

                    Your political views................ -6
                    Your educational background......... -7
                    Your unwillingness to conform....... -8
                    Your attitudes toward authority..... -9
                    None of these....................... -0

 e. Generally do you think it'll be easy, pretty hard or practically impossible to accept the kinds of options offered to people like yourself by the Establishment?

                                        Easy...........67-1
                                        Pretty hard..... -2
                                        Impossible...... -3
                                        Not sure........ -4

16. (SHOW CARD M) To be even more specific, which of the following
restraints imposed by society and its institutions can you accept
easily, which do you accept reluctantly, and which do you reject
outright?

	Accept Easily	Accept Reluctantly	Reject Outright
Abiding by laws you don't agree with....	68-1	-2	-3
Conforming in matters of dress and personal grooming.......................	69-1	-2	-3
Keeping your views to yourself..........	70-1	-2	-3
Outward conformity for the sake of career advancement......................	71-1	-2	-3
The power and authority of the "boss" in a work situation.....................	72-1	-2	-3
Living like everyone else..............	73-1	-2	-3
Settling down to a routine.............	74-1	-2	-3
The prohibition against marijuana.......	75-1	-2	-3
The prohibition against mind-expansion drugs.........................	76-1	-2	-3
The prohibition against heroin..........	77-1	-2	-3
The power and authority of the police...	78-1	-2	-3

                                                            80-3

VI - STUDENT RADICALISM

17a Do you feel that student radicalism is continuing to grow, leveling off or declining?

Continuing to grow..... 5-1
Leveling off........... -2
Declining.............. -3
Not sure............... -4

b. (SHOW CARD N) Which of the tactics on this card do you feel are always justifiable, which are sometimes justifiable, and which do you feel are never justifiable?

	Always	Some-times	Never
Sit-ins..	6-1	-2	-3
Ultimatums to those in authority.................	7-1	-2	-3
Blockades of buildings............................	8-1	-2	-3
Destruction or mutilation of property............	9-1	-2	-3
Bombing or setting fires to buildings owned by large corporations or the military..........	10-1	-2	-3
Destroying draft board records...................	11-1	-2	-3
Resisting or disobeying police...................	12-1	-2	-3
Assaulting police................................	13-1	-2	-3
Holding an authority captive.....................	14-1	-2	-3
Providing sanctuary for "political" prisoners....	15-1	-2	-3

18. (HAND CARD O) Which of these statements best expresses your feelings about the use of violence?

1. Violent means are often necessary..........................16-1

2. Violence is justified--but only when all else fails......... -2

3. I am opposed to violence.................................... -3

210

TECHNICAL DETAILS OF THE SURVEY

19. (SHOW CARD P) Which of these comes closest to your own point of view? (CALL OFF THE LETTERS AND NAME AS MANY AS YOU WANT) The best methods for achieving meaningful social change in the country are:

    a. Mobilizing the pressures of public opinion......................17-1

    b. New government legislation, rigorously enforced................ -2

    c. Changing the method of selecting candidates for public office in the two major parties................................ -3

    d. Organizing a new major political party......................... -4

    e. Changing the values and consciousness of those in positions of power... -5

    f. Creating the objective conditions for revolution.............. -6

    g. Adopting tactics of harassment and confrontation.............. -7

    h. Forcing those in power to adopt repressive measures to expose them.. -8

    i. Each individual doing all he can do to effect change in his own community and the organizations in which he is personally involved... -9

    j. Changing the basic values and outlook of the public............ -0

    k. Organizing those who are now excluded from effective participation and power--the poor, the ethnic minorities, youth, etc...18-1

    l. Creating greater class consciousness among workers............. -2

    m. Working within the system, like Ralph Nader, to expose the unresponsiveness of the system................................ -3

    n. Respecting the police and other authorities................... -4

    o. Decentralizing power from the federal government to the local government.. -5

    p. Cracking down on draft resisters.............................. -6

    q. Giving the local community more power and control and taking it away from the large, centralized bureaucracies....... -7

    r. Creating more respect for law and order.......................19-1

    s. Nationalizing the resources of the country.................... -2

    t. Nationalizing private industry in order to eliminate the profit motive.. -3

    u. Cracking down on welfare cheaters............................. -4

    v. Letting things continue just as they are...................... -5

    w. Having more respect for the flag.............................. -6

APPENDIX

20. Do you agree or disagree with the idea that:

	Agree	Disagree
Most men live lives of quiet desperation.............	20-1	21-1
Very little of what we read in newspapers and magazines or see on TV can be trusted................	-2	-2
A person can no longer automatically assume that there will be a future; the threat of destruction by atomic warfare or pollution life on this planet hangs by a thread.....................................	-3	-3
If the purpose is morally justified, it may be necessary to use people as tools to accomplish the goals..	-4	-4

21. (SHOW CARD Q) If you had to make a choice, which <u>one</u> of these two statements best describes your views?

    A. Our present system of government is largely democratic. Sooner or later the views of the people make themselves felt in important matters......................................22-1

OR

    B. Our present system of government is democratic in name only. The special interests run things and the mass of people are propagandized that what they think really counts........... -2

VIII - IDENTIFICATION/ALIENATION

22a. In general do you feel that your personal values and point of view are shared by most Americans today?

                                                     Yes.............23-1
                                                   Not certain..... -2
                                                   No............. -3

  b How about your fellow students--do you feel that your personal values and point of view are shared by most of your fellow students?

                                                      Yes.............24-1
                                                   Not certain..... -2
                                                   No............. -3

  c. Do you think your values and point of view are represented by our government?

                                                      Yes............25-1
                                                   No............. -2
                                                   Not sure....... -3

23.   (SHOW CARD R) With which of the following groups, if any, do you feel
      a sense of identification?

A.	The middle class........................	26-1
B.	The working class.......................	-2
C.	Students................................	-3
D.	The New Left............................	-4
E.	Conservatives...........................	-5
F.	The Old Left............................	-6
G.	Liberals................................	-7
H.	People of your nationality..............	-8
I.	People of your religion.................	-9
J.	Other people of your own generation......	-0
K.	The Movement............................	27-1
L.	People of your race.....................	-2
M.	People in your neighborhood.............	-3
N.	Your family.............................	-4
O.	The counter-culture.....................	-5

80-4

The section that follows contains graphic summaries of selected tables previously presented in the text. Cross references are clearly indicated. For *quick* appraisal of particular student reactions, the various bar graphs and pie segments should prove useful.

Phrases Which Best Describe
Current Student Mood

Total Students 1971

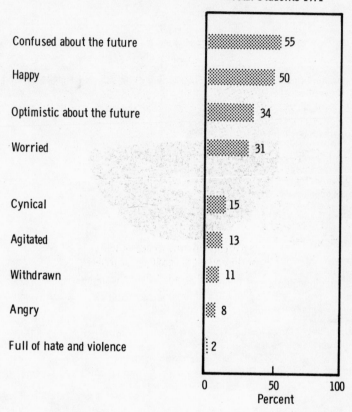

	Percent
Confused about the future	55
Happy	50
Optimistic about the future	34
Worried	31
Cynical	15
Agitated	13
Withdrawn	11
Angry	8
Full of hate and violence	2

Also see Table 1 on page 22

Students Contrast Their Present Mood
With How They Felt Last Year

Q. Are You More or Less. . . .

Total Students 1971

Involved in your own private life & concerns

Concerned about what's happening in Vietn.

Happy in your own personal life

Skeptical about Government honesty

Fearful about employment in the future

Serious about studying

Willing to participate in protests

Confident about underlying health of Ctry.

Alienated from the society

Conserv. in your polit. thinking

Accepting violence as a legit. tactic.

-60   0   +60

Percent

Also see Table 2 on page 23

216

Student Views About Whether
Campus Radicalism is Growing or Declining

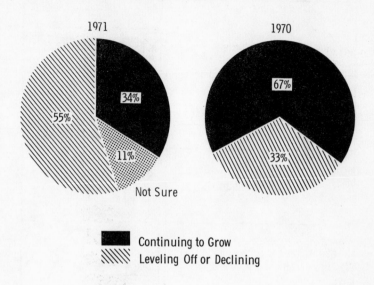

1971

1970

34%

55%

11%

Not Sure

67%

33%

■ Continuing to Grow
\\\\\\\ Leveling Off or Declining

Also see Table 4 on page 24

Also see Table 5 on page 34

Acceptance of Social Restraints

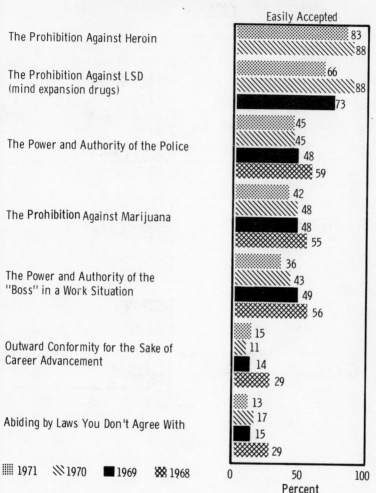

Easily Accepted

The Prohibition Against Heroin — 83 / 88

The Prohibition Against LSD (mind expansion drugs) — 66 / 88 / 73

The Power and Authority of the Police — 45 / 45 / 48 / 59

The Prohibition Against Marijuana — 42 / 48 / 48 / 55

The Power and Authority of the "Boss" in a Work Situation — 36 / 43 / 49 / 56

Outward Conformity for the Sake of Career Advancement — 15 / 11 / 14 / 29

Abiding by Laws You Don't Agree With — 13 / 17 / 15 / 29

1971   1970   1969   1968

0   50   100

Percent

Also see Table 6 on page 35

219

Activities Seen As Morally Wrong

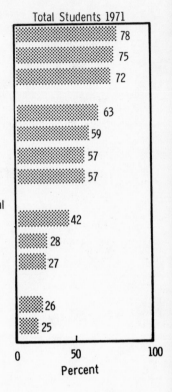

Activities Morally Wrong	Total Students 1971
Taking things without paying for them	78
Collecting welfare when you could work	75
Destroying private property	72
Paying one's way through college by selling dope	63
Interchanging partners among couples	59
Breaking the law	57
Extramarital sexual relations	57
Planning and having children without formal marriage	42
Leaving the country to avoid the draft	28
Having an abortion	27
Relations between consenting homosexuals	26
Casual/premarital sexual relationships	25

Percent

Also see Table 7 on page 37

Values Important in One's Life

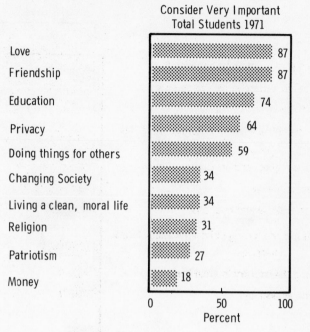

Consider Very Important
Total Students 1971

	Percent
Love	87
Friendship	87
Education	74
Privacy	64
Doing things for others	59
Changing Society	34
Living a clean, moral life	34
Religion	31
Patriotism	27
Money	18

Also see Table 8 on page 37

Extent of Belief in Traditional Values

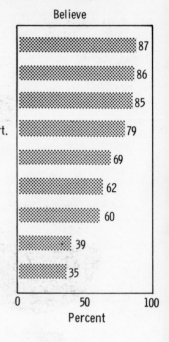

Believe

Children should respect parents	87
Society needs legally based authority	86
Business entitled to profit	85
Commitment to a meaningful career is import.	79
The right to private property sacred	69
Competion encourages excellence	62
With strength of character a person can control what happens to him	60
Hard work always pays off	39
Organized religion is important	35

0   50   100

Percent

Also see Table 9 on page 40

Extent of Belief in Traditional Values

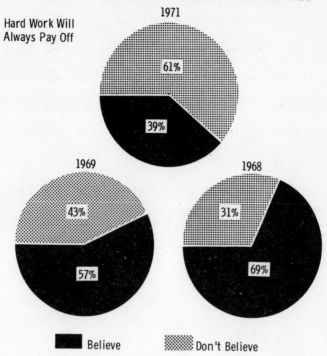

Hard Work Will
Always Pay Off

1971

61%

39%

1969

43%

57%

1968

31%

69%

■ Believe   ▦ Don't Believe

Also see Table 9 on page 41

223

Is Marriage Obsolete?

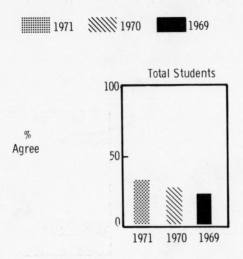

Also see Table 11 on page 43

Interest in Living in Collectives, Communes or Off The Land

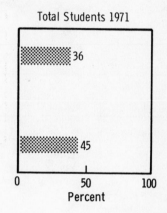

Total Students 1971

Interested in Living
in a Commune   36

Interested in Living
Off the Land   45

0   50   100

Percent

Also see Table 15 and 16 on page 45

225

Career Minded Students and Those Who Take Affluence For Granted

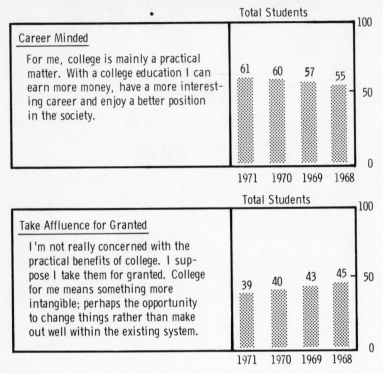

Total Students

Career Minded

For me, college is mainly a practical matter. With a college education I can earn more money, have a more interesting career and enjoy a better position in the society.

61 60 57 55

1971 1970 1969 1968

Total Students

Take Affluence for Granted

I'm not really concerned with the practical benefits of college. I suppose I take them for granted. College for me means something more intangible; perhaps the opportunity to change things rather than make out well within the existing system.

39 40 43 45

1971 1970 1969 1968

Also see Table 17 on page 46

Self-Doubts About Making Money

 1971  1970  1969

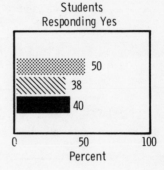

Students
Responding Yes

Have Self-Doubts
About Making Money

50

38

40

0   50   100
Percent

Also see Table 18 on page 47

Influences on Career Choice

1971 ░░░░   ▨▨▨ 1970

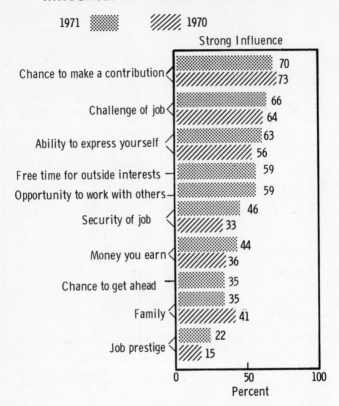

Strong Influence

Chance to make a contribution — 70 / 73

Challenge of job — 66 / 64

Ability to express yourself — 63 / 56

Free time for outside interests — 59

Opportunity to work with others — 59

Security of job — 46 / 33

Money you earn — 44 / 36

Chance to get ahead — 35

Family — 35 / 41

Job prestige — 22 / 15

0   50   100

Percent

Also see Table 19 on page 47

Barriers Toward Getting Work

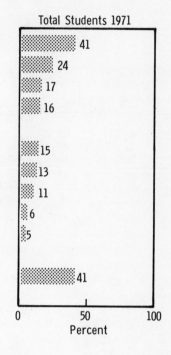

Total Students 1971

Your Attitude Towards Authority — 41
Your Unwillingness to Conform — 24
Your Educational Background — 17
Your Sex — 16

Your Political Views — 15
Your Style of Dress — 13
Your Race — 11
Your Family Background — 6
Your Religion — 5

None of These — 41

0   50   100
Percent

Also see Table 20 on page 48

If The Vietnam War Were To End Today...

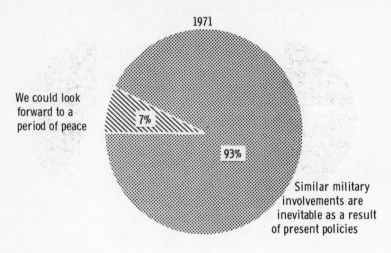

1971

We could look
forward to a
period of peace

7%

93%

Similar military
involvements are
inevitable as a result
of present policies

Also see Table 22 on page 61

Are We a "Sick Society"?

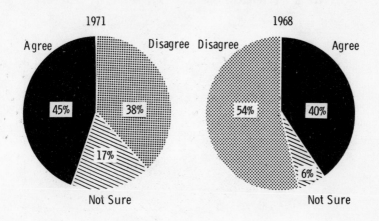

1971

Agree   Disagree   Disagree   Agree

45%   38%   54%   40%

17%   6%

Not Sure   Not Sure

1968

Also see Table 24 on page 61

231

Extent of Agreement With
Criticisms Made About American Society

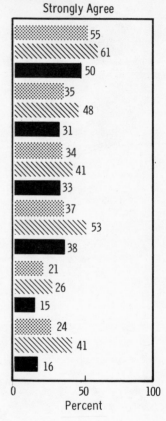

Business is too concerned with profits
not public responsibility

Our foreign policy is based on our own
narrow economic and power interests

Economic well-being in this country is
unjustly and unfairly distributed

Basically we are a racist nation

Today's American society is characterized by injustice, insensibility, lack
of candor and inhumanity

The war in Vietnam is pure
Imperialism

Also see Table 25 on page 62

232

The Most Significant Signs That Things Are Not Working Properly

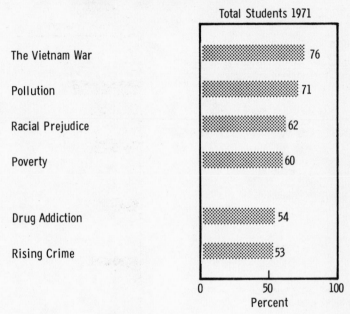

Total Students 1971

The Vietnam War   76

Pollution   71

Racial Prejudice   62

Poverty   60

Drug Addiction   54

Rising Crime   53

0   50   100

Percent

Also see Table 26 on page 65

Where the Real Power in The Country is Vested

'The Real Power in the Country Lies With:

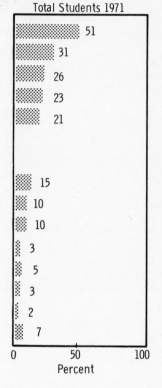

	Total Students 1971
The giant corporation	51
Congress	31
Financiers and financial institutions	26
The President	23
The Defense Department	21
The interplay of diverse special interest groups, such as labor, religious leaders and educators	15
The general public	10
The CIA	10
The Democratic party	3
The technocrats	5
The Republican party	3
Other	2
Not sure	7

Percent

Also see Table 27 on page 67

Whether or Not We Have
a Real Democracy

Our present system
of government is
largely democratic.
Sooner or later
the views of the
people make
themselves felt.

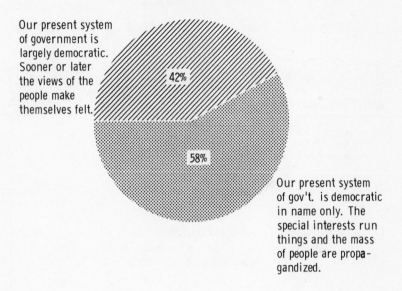

Our present system
of gov't. is democratic
in name only. The
special interests run
things and the mass
of people are propa-
gandized.

Also see Table 28 on page 67

Attitudes Toward American Society and Way Of Life

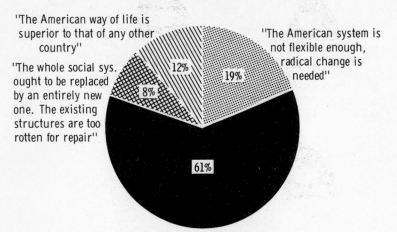

"The American way of life is superior to that of any other country"

"The whole social sys. ought to be replaced by an entirely new one. The existing structures are too rotten for repair"

8%

12%

19%

"The American system is not flexible enough, radical change is needed"

61%

"There are serious flaws in our society today, but the system is flexible enough to solve them"

Also see Table 29 on page 68

Institutions That Most Need Changes–1971

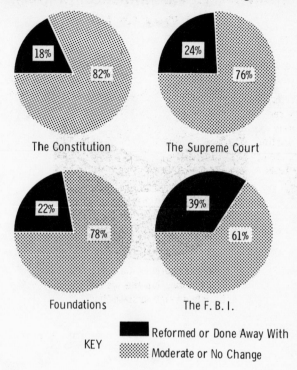

The Constitution   The Supreme Court

Foundations   The F. B. I.

KEY   Reformed or Done Away With
     Moderate or No Change

Also see Table 32 on page 71

237

Institutions That Most Need Change
(Continued)

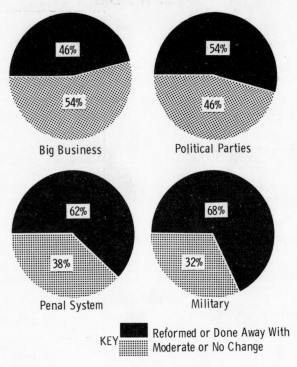

Big Business

Political Parties

Penal System

Military

KEY ▬ Reformed or Done Away With
░░░ Moderate or No Change

Also see Table 32 on page 72

238

Social Problems to Whose Solution the Student is Willing to Commit a Year or Two of His Life

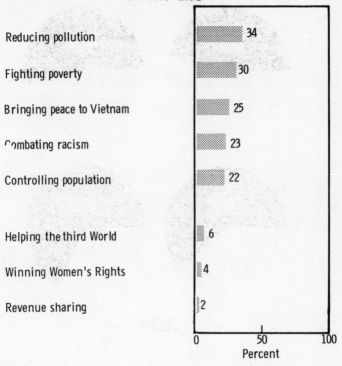

Also see Table 34 on page 74

Best Methods For Achieving
Meaningful Social Change

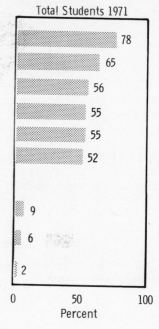

Total Students 1971

Individual doing what he
can in community — 78

Working within the system — 65

Pressures of public opinion — 56

Changing values and outlook of public — 55

Organize minorities now excluded — 55

Change values of those in power — 52

Force those in power to adopt
repressive measures and expose them — 9

Adopt tactics of harassment
and confrontation — 6

Let things continue as they are — 2

0   50   100
Percent

Also see Table 35 on page 75

Is it Best to Work Outside or Inside The System?

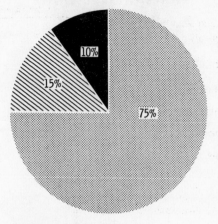

■ Outside the System
▦ Within the System
▧ Not Sure

Also see Table 36 on page 76

Personal Preference for Working With The Establishment or The Protest Movement

▒ 1971   ▨ 1970

Prefer To Work With:

Total Students

Protest Movement
▒ 19
▨ 18

Establishment
▒ 53
▨ 49

No Difference
or Neither
▒ 27
▨ 32

0   50   100

Percent

Also see Table 37 on page 76

Voter Registration and Intentions to Vote

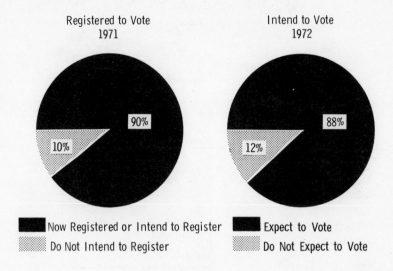

Registered to Vote
1971

Intend to Vote
1972

90%

10%

88%

12%

Now Registered or Intend to Register

Do Not Intend to Register

Expect to Vote

Do Not Expect to Vote

Also see Table 43 on page 81

Self-Identification as Conservative, Moderate, Liberal or Radical

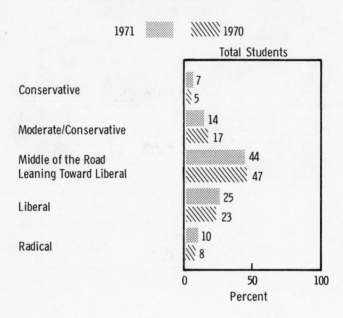

1971 ▦   ⧄⧄⧄ 1970

Total Students

Conservative
- 7
- 5

Moderate/Conservative
- 14
- 17

Middle of the Road
Leaning Toward Liberal
- 44
- 47

Liberal
- 25
- 23

Radical
- 10
- 8

0   50   100

Percent

Also see Table 44 on page 81

244

Self-Identification With Political Parties

 1971   \\\ 1970   ■ 1969

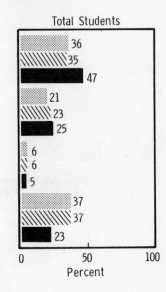

Total Students

Democratic
36
35
47

Republican
21
23
25

Other
6
6
5

None
37
37
23

0   50   100
Percent

Also see Table 45 on page 82

Acceptance of Life Styles
Offered By The Society

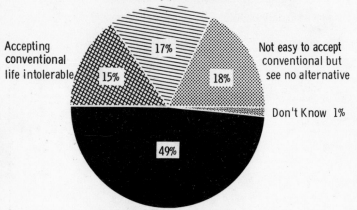

Just about the same kind
of life as my parents have

Accepting
conventional
life intolerable

17%

Not easy to accept
conventional but
see no alternative

15%

18%

Don't Know 1%

49%

No great difficulty in accepting
conventional life, good job, marriage
living in suburbs, etc.

Also see Table 50 on page 88